OUT OF THIS WORLD

OUT OF THIS WORLD
The Natural History of Milton Acorn

CHRIS GUDGEON

ARSENAL PULP PRESS
Vancouver

OUT OF THIS WORLD
Copyright © 1996 by Chris Gudgeon

ARSENAL PULP PRESS
103-1014 Homer Street
Vancouver, B.C.
Canada v6b 2w9

The publisher gratefully acknowledges the assistance of the Canada Council and the Cultural Services Branch, B.C. Ministry of Small Business, Tourism and Culture.

Poems and prose by Milton Acorn reprinted with permission by the Milton Acorn Estate.
Photographs, unless otherwise indicated, reprinted with permission by Mary Hooper.
An earlier version of David McFadden's foreword appeared in *Canadian Notes & Queries*.
Excerpt from *Echoes from Labour's Wars* reprinted with permission by Don MacGillvray.
Excerpt from *Reaching for the Beaufort Sea* by Al Purdy reprinted with permission by
   Harbour Publishing.
Typeset by the Vancouver Desktop Publishing Centre
Printed and bound in Canada by Kromar Printing

CANADIAN CATALOGUING IN PUBLICATION DATA:
Gudgeon, Chris, 1959-
   Out of this world

   Includes index.
   ISBN 1-55152-030-3
   1. Acorn, Milton, 1923-1986—Biography. 2. Poets, Canadian (English)—20th
century—Biography.* I. Title.
ps8501.c8z7 1996   c811'.54   c96-910032-9
pr9199.3.a18z7 1996

Contents

Acknowledgements

Thanks to:

Milt's family: Garth Hooper, David Hooper, Kay Traynor, Robert Acorn, and Vimy Gregory, the Acorn family historian. Special thanks to Mary Hooper, Milt's sister; without her tireless efforts this book never would have been published.

Milt's friends and colleagues, including bill bissett, John Robert Colombo, Melany Cleveland, Christopher Dewdney, Louis Dudek, Chris Faiers, Marty Floman, Michael Gnarowski, Bill Howell, Christopher Hyde, Arlene Lampert, Valerie LaPointe, Dennis Lee, Dan McLeod, Don MacLeod, Kent Martin, Gabor Maté, Robin Matthews, Robert Priest, Peter Shama, Raymond Souster, Rosemary Sullivan, Sylvia Tyson, Joyce Wayne, Robert Weaver, and David Woodhead. Special thanks to George Bowering, Douglas Fetherling, Patrick Lane, David McFadden, Al Purdy, and Cedric Smith. This book could not have been written without James Deahl, Milt's unofficial literary executor, who supplied me with numerous contacts and other information, and Joe Rosenblatt, who supplied stories, advice and moral support.

The Canada Council, for a grant which enabled me to write this book, Gail Donald at the CBC Archives, and the National Archives of Canada, in particular Anne Goddard, for their invaluable assistance.

My friends and colleagues in the publishing world, especially the people at Arsenal Pulp Press (Brian Lam, Steve Osborne, Blaine Kyllo, Kevin Barefoot, Linda Field, and Dennis Priebe) and my literary agent Daphne Hart.

My friends and family, especially my wonderful wife Barb Stewart, our three boys Tavish, Charlie, and Keating, and my mother, Pat Gudgeon.

For Tony Nelson

Foreword

by David McFadden

WHEN I FIRST MET MILTON ACORN, he and Gwendolyn MacEwen were married and living on Ward's Island. They were devoted and tried hard but it didn't last long. Acorn was a rather unusual fellow, even for a poet. He visited me at home twice, and since I was still living with my parents, I couldn't have been more than twenty. My father was quite intrigued with this fellow who looked like the original for the cartoon character Alley Oop. He liked him, in spite of the fact that Acorn at one point brazenly took an expensive cigar out of my father's shirt pocket, unwrapped it, stuck it in his mouth and asked for a light. "I like this brand," he said.

Actually, I think that was what my father really liked about Acorn. He still remembers this incident now, with a happy smile, at eighty-two. And yes, he did give him the light.

I took Acorn up to the Mountain Brow, affording a spectacular view of Hamilton, Ontario, and half of Lake Ontario. He stood there looking down at the city, waving his fists and shouting, "Wake up! Wake up!" This was in the middle of the afternoon. I was a pretty naïve young fellow, and a bit embarrassed. I thought of all the steelworkers and hospital staff on the night shift snoring away and hoped his loud voice wasn't disturbing their much-needed sleep. Acorn's neck was red and bulging with big thick veins as he shouted down at the nice people of my little city. It didn't occur to me at the time that this was Milton's own Sermon on the Mount. "Wake up!"

Years later, long after MacEwen and Acorn had separated, I found myself driving Acorn in my Volkswagen van to a poetry reading in Guelph. As we, two guys from Prince Edward Island, drove along, I started playing my Stompin' Tom Connors tapes to calm him down. He was attentive to the music for a while, but soon I could hear him whispering very softly to himself: "Would you care to have lunch with me? I'll pay. How about lunch? It's on me." And so on, over and over. He seemed to be practicing for a formal invitation, but it never came, no matter how hard he tried to get the words right.

The reading was set for Wednesday, but this was Sunday. Guelph seemed deserted as I dropped him off at the main downtown corner.

"What are you going to do 'til Wednesday?" I asked.

"I'll think of something," he said.

As I drove off, he looked like a terribly lonely saint in the rear view mirror. I should have taken him to lunch, but there were some other pressing obligations in my way—as there always were in those busy days of youthful ignorance.

At one of my little lunches with MacEwen just before her death, we got talking about Acorn. He had died several years earlier in Charlottetown, where he was widely known and loved. I screwed up my courage and raised the sensitive issue of Acorn's peculiar body odour. Acorn was one of those people who always had a strange smell about him. Kind of unbearable, actually. Everyone knew it but no one ever said anything. I asked MacEwen how she could stand it, being married to him and all. She said she couldn't.

"Oh, I tell you," she said, "it drove me crazy. I would take all his clothes off, put him in the tub and scrub him with soap from head to foot. And when he got out I would have all fresh clothes for him. And he would smell just as bad."

I told her about the time Acorn had a terrible case of hay fever. This was at a party at Arlene Lampert's place, back in the days when Arlene and her late husband Gerry were always throwing splendid parties for poets. Acorn was a much more public boozehound than MacEwen ever was, but he was on the wagon at the time. His nose and eyes were running and he was obviously in a lot of misery. I asked him if he was taking anything for his hay fever and it soon became obvious he had no idea there was anything to be taken for this miserable condition. He had never heard of antihistamines.

Acorn was a poet who just didn't know a lot of ordinary things about life. He didn't know where to get milk, as someone once said about someone else. Acorn was a friend of the late Selwyn Dewdney and his wife Irene, and he used to visit them in their large house in London, Ontario on occasion, and stay as long as he could. Their son, Christopher, who is now a widely respected poet, was a kid at the time, and remembers going into the kitchen early one morning and finding Acorn, with one eye shut, carefully pouring milk into the electric kettle.

"What are you doing, Mr. Acorn?" little Christopher asked.

"Making hot chocolate, kid," Acorn said.

So, at Arlene's party, I offered to take Acorn down to the pharmacy to get him some antihistamines. I sat in the car as Acorn went into the pharmacy. When he came out he had a little bottle of pills in his hand and a big smile on his unforgettably craggy face. In fact, he was beaming.

"I am so famous, it's amazing," he said. "Everywhere I go in this country people recognize me. In the east, in the west, even in Ontario. Even the pharmacist. I paid for the pills and he said thank you, Mr. Acorn." Acorn was famous for his passionate, powerful verse: he was the People's Poet, and he had Tasted his Blood. But his fame was enhanced by his unforgettable personal appearance. Once seen, never forgotten.

I was in a terribly devilish mood by now. I don't know why, but I always liked to pester Acorn a little, in a genial way really, not to provoke a fight but just to keep the spirits alive. I somehow always had the feeling of anonymity and invisibility when I was around him, so powerful was his presence.

"It's not fair," I said. "Take a guy like me. I'm a much better poet than you, but no one ever recognizes me."

I really didn't care about being recognized, and was merely making a joke, but it was a nervy joke, because Acorn had a terrible temper and a high regard, naturally, for his own poetry. In fact, in a filmed interview once, he was asked if he thought his poetry would be read after he was long gone. "I'm betting my life on it," he said.

As for his hot temper, I'd seen him screaming at someone one night over beer at the now-defunct Collingwood Poetry Festival. The poor recipient of his rage had probably said something far less offensive than what I'd just hit him with. The veins in Acorn's neck were bulging. "I'll break all the little bones in your face," he was screaming.

But Acorn was in a sweet mood in spite of his allergies, and my comment didn't bother him at all. He realized it was a joke. But he had one better. He turned with a quizzical look and said, "Who *are* you, anyway?"

I told him that we'd known each other for a long time; I'd been to his house on Ward's Island, I'd driven him to Guelph, we had many friends in common, he'd met my father and stolen cigars from him, and so on.

"Oh, you're David McFadden!" he shouted. He then paused for a moment and said, "You're right, you *are* a better poet than I am. That piece you did about the Micmacs of Prince Edward Island, that was a helluva good poem."

When we got back to Arlene and Gerry's party, Acorn took a couple of antihistamines and quickly stopped snorting and sniffling. I'd never seen him so happy—and grateful. It was as if I'd removed a thorn from his paw. Towards the end of the evening he came up with a sheet of paper in his hand and shyly handed it to me. In red ink he had written:

> This document gives David McFadden all rights in perpe-
> tuity to poach on my preserves whenever and in any way he
> sees fit.   (signed) Milton Acorn

I was mightily impressed. Such generosity was rare among poets in any age. I had the document framed and hanging on the wall for a season or two. Unfortunately it was opposite a south window. I went away for the summer and when I got back Acorn's words had faded into nothingness.

I've never met anyone like Acorn, not even in books. In a land that tends to worship sameness, Acorn was an amazing anomaly. He was a strange, brilliant, wild, original, complicated, at times silly, at times stinky, and always tremendously interesting man, so much so that steps must be taken to prevent him from being forgotten. I'm thrilled that *Out of This World* will shed much-needed light on this gentle monster from our immediate past.

(An Invocation)
 The needle on the dial points to death
Which may be soon or late
More likely soon than late
So I'd better finish it
Write my autobiography
Paying attention to truth; for these
So to speak, are dying words
            —Introduction to Milton Acorn's
                unfinished autobiography

INTRODUCTION

Out of this World

I'm out of this world—I'm in
Either here or in the mirror on the wall
For my curious critical drinking eyes
For you in this neat book or the clang of vibrations in sight, in sound;
By this blade stamped and honed I decree
I shall be another man to you, my description confounded . . .
    —"On Shaving Off His Beard," unpublished

IN THE FALL OF 1992 MY WIFE BARB AND I were still fresh in Toronto and I was obsessed with Stan Rogers. I was half-way into my research on a book about the folk singer, who died in an Air Canada fire in 1984, and would spend the entire day at the Metro Toronto Reference Library, only to come home and sit in my little office, pour over my notes and listen to Stan Rogers' cassettes again and again on my tiny mono tape recorder. I had bought *The Stan Rogers Songbook*, and struggled to learn a number of songs ("The Mary Ellen Carter," "Free in the Harbour") on my untunable twelve-string guitar; I—who after thirty-seven years, have yet to memorize my own mother's birth date—committed all nine verses of "Barrett's Privateers" to memory. One day, Barb brought me a book from HarperCollins, the publishing house

19

where she worked as a kind of editorial assistant. It was a collection of essays called *Living in a Dark Age* by *The Globe & Mail* social commentator Rick Salutin, and it was here that I found my next obsession.

The book's title came from "Knowing I Live in a Dark Age," a poem I'd never read, written by a man I'd never heard of, a poet with the unlikely, perfect name of Milton Acorn. I assumed it was a clever pen name—when Earle Birney first heard it he thought it was Al Purdy's clever pen name—but soon found out that the name was real and that it belonged to a man who was both a magnificent writer and a fascinating character. As I began to look into his life, I discovered that Acorn was a mystery; a walking, talking, cigar smoking question mark, who—like Rogers—had great artistic gifts which barely outweighed his capacity for both anger and compassion. Milt was born on The Island. That's what he called it. Not Prince Edward Island, which was a nod to the forces of Imperialism Milton abhorred. And not, by God, P.E.I.; pronounced "Pee-eye" by Islanders, it sounded like a mild expletive, and Milton was not one for mild expletives. He liked his swear words full and frothy, unequivocally obscene, for he was not a man of half-measures. He swore by Marx's theory of dialectics, lived his own life swinging between the poles of Love and Anger. Milt was born on The Island years ago, but had spent most of his life elsewhere: Montreal, Toronto, Vancouver and points in between. He left The Island, like so many young men, to seek his fortune and fame, and returned, like so many old men, to die.

Throughout his life Milt was fascinated with the man in the mirror. While many artists carefully construct a public image to protect their private lives, time, talent and circumstance invented the poet Milton Acorn, and he tried to hammer together a private life that suited this image. Toward that end, he was constantly refining the details of his life until the simplest facts were obscured. Was he a native Indian? Were his parents from the working class? Did he have a steel plate in his head? Even his exact birth date is in some doubt; in my research I found three different dates. Milt told so many versions of his life that it's almost impossible to tell where reality ends and the reflection begins. On top of this, many of his medical, military and personal records are not available for public scrutiny—which makes the job of writing a "definitive biography" impossible. At times I felt like a detective, sifting through the contradictory stories and scant evidence, searching for shards of the real Milton Acorn among the mirror images.

Acorn is a man whose life is shrouded in mystery, but the biggest mystery of all is, what happened to Milton Acorn? In the early 1970s he was one of the most famous poets in the country, right up there with Layton, Purdy, Cohen and Atwood. His readings regularly sold out—that's right, in the early seventies people often *paid* to hear poets —while one of his books sold 10,000 copies, which put him in the same league as Robert Service. He was co-founder of Vancouver's alternative paper *The Georgia Straight*, which is still going strong twenty years later, and was a charter member of the folk group Perth County Conspiracy, whose leader Cedric Smith set several of Milt's poems to music. But Acorn wasn't just a popular artist, he was one of the greatest poets this country has ever produced; his best ten poems stack up to anything written in the English language in the last fifty years. Like Stan Rogers, Milt set out to change the Canadian cultural landscape; Acorn fought the academic and political forces which were determined to keep our colonial mindset in place. Before Milton Acorn, and his close friend Al Purdy, there were no professional poets in this country; schoolchildren were weaned on Yeats and Emerson and Burns. Today, thanks in no small part to Milton Acorn, Canadian anthologies are being used in schools around the country, and universities around the world offer Canadian Literature courses. Meanwhile, people write poems. Some even make a living at it.

Sadly though, as the lot of the professional poet has advanced, the memory of Milton Acorn and his poems has faded. Most of his books are out of print, while those still available are published by small presses with limited distribution (although his excellent collection *Dig Up My Heart* was recently rereleased as part of McClelland & Stewart's Modern Canadian Poets Series). High school teachers and university professors rarely teach Acorn's poems, even in CanLit survey courses, and where it was once unthinkable to put together an anthology without including at least a few of Acorn's chestnuts, today's anthologists get along without any at all. It's a shame, for Milton Acorn's life and legacy flies in the face of that too-Canadian belief that artists are boring and second-rate. He was a fascinating contradiction: at times petty and inane, at times brilliant, larger than life. This book then is part biography, part mystery, part literary history, part poetry primer, but most of all a celebration of the man who often teetered on the edge of madness, and the poems that lifted him out of this world into the realm of genius.

CHAPTER ONE

Island Born

Take this Island now.
A cradle it is:
Small enough to rock
Before the fireplace
On a homey evening—
All red and green and gentle.
　　　　　—Untitled, unpublished

PRINCE EDWARD ISLAND IS RED. Of course, everyone knows that. But you don't realize exactly *how* red it is until you see The Island come into view through the airplane window. That's when you see there's nothing quite like The Island anywhere else in the world. I come from an island myself, Vancouver Island—or to be precise, Victoria, which is an island unto itself—and I appreciate the effect that geography can have on people. Islanders tend to be independent, to speak their minds, and are always anchored by a nagging awareness of their limitations. "If you want to know what Islanders are," Milt Acorn wrote in his Governor General's Award-winning *The Island Means Minago*, "the first thing to understand is, some are, some aren't." In other words, you can be born and raised on an island, but not have the Island temperament. Likewise, you don't have to live on an island to be an Islander, as Milton's case proves. The longer he stayed away, the more of an Islander he became, until, like Victoria, he was an Island unto himself, not a hermit, but a distinct society within confederation, Canada's unofficial eleventh province.

I went to Prince Edward Island to visit Milt's brother Robert Acorn and his sister Mary Hooper, to try and get a better sense of the man whose life I'd decided to impose upon. I rented a car at the Charlottetown airport and drove to the Hooper farm some four miles outside of the provincial capital. On my way, I cruised through the city, a clean town, newly renovated with an old façade, a tourist town like Victoria. Over the last ten years, Charlottetown has become a popular holiday spot, thanks in part to a curious obsession that young Japanese women have developed for Anne of Green Gables—Anne with Red Hair, they call her—the feisty P.E.I.-based heroine of Lucy Maud Montgomery's children's books. Japanese girls arrive in Charlottetown by the planeload and take a charter bus to visit Green Gables in Cavendish, and to watch the musical version of *Anne* at the Confederation Centre Theatre in Charlottetown. They are fascinated with the story of the independent orphan who succeeds in a male-dominated world. Milt liked Anne too. Once at an Alcoholics Anonymous meeting, Milt told Toronto playwright Tom Walmsley that if he was stuck on a desert island he'd want three books with him: the "Big Book" (A.A.'s 12-step guide), *The Communist Manifesto*, and Lucy Maud Montgomery's *Anne of Green Gables*.

The Hooper farm is a twenty-minute drive from town, along a highway that quickly moves from urban to rural. I marveled that The Island is a province at all. John Robert Colombo's *Canadian Global Almanac* says that P.E.I. has a population just under 130,000 — 100,000 less than live in Victoria, in an area roughly the same as metropolitan Toronto. If P.E.I. were the standard, Canada would have fifty provinces or more. The Island also preserves a mix of conservative and progressive thinking: as a province, P.E.I. has the lowest divorce rate next to Newfoundland, while it has by far the highest number of students per capita enrolled in French immersion. And to hear Milton Acorn tell it, The Island has long been a hotbed for revolutionaries.

"The Island is supposed to be distinguished by having no history at all, except the Charlottetown Conference where Confederation was conceived, though not born," Milt wrote in his introduction to *The Island Means Minago*. "The location of the Charlottetown Conference was no accident. Nothing is. It was absolutely necessary for the British Imperialists, if they wanted to pass off their proposed pseudo-nationhood in preference for a real nationhood for Canada, to bring The Island in."

It was into this curious environment that Milton James Rhode Acorn was born on March 30, 1923, in the midst of a late winter snowstorm. But like The Island itself, which officially entered into existence as a province on July 1, 1873, you have to turn to history to fully appreciate the myth and meaning of Milton Acorn. While the surname seems a little strange to mainland ears, on The Island it's common enough, and in fact the Acorn family tree has firm roots in North America. The original "Eichorn" was a miller from Prussia named Matthias, who immigrated to Maine in 1748. His son was Matthias Jr., and he was married twice, the second time, according to Acorn family historian Vimy Gregory, of Winsloe, P.E.I., to a native woman who was the source of the stories of "Indian blood" that run through the family. Around the time of the American Revolution, the family anglicized the name to Acorn and one of them, John, made his way to Prince Edward Island. He'd been granted land on The Island as a reward for fighting against the American rebels. It's odd this second generation American would side with the English, especially since most of his relatives joined the revolutionary army. One story has it that, being the eldest son of the eldest son, John stood to inherit the family legacy, so a cunning uncle had him inducted into the British army.

But the Acorns have a habit of defying authority and going their own way; maybe old John was just carrying on in the revolutionary tradition. John had at least thirteen children, and numerous grand- and great-grandchildren including Gilbert Chester Acorn, who moved his family to Sydney on Cape Breton Island. He got into some financial trouble selling shares for a silver fox company; when the company went bankrupt, Chester was left holding the bag, and had to return to P.E.I. with his fortunes diminished. Still, the family was well respected.

His maternal grandmother was Martha Jago, the first female preacher this side of the Atlantic. Gilbert's one brother Morley was mayor of nearby Surrey, and another brother, Herbert, was a member of the provincial legislature. Gilbert Acorn married Mary Ellen Fairclough. Originally, the Faircloughs were a well-to-do family from Britain. Some of the younger sons emigrated to The Island, but their boat sank along the way. Two of the young men died and all the family papers were destroyed, leaving the survivors unable to prove any claims they had to an inheritance. Together, Gilbert Acorn and Mary Fairclough had five daughters and one son, Milton's father Robert, who was born late in 1896.

While the Acorn side of the family gave Milt a sense of history, his mother's ancestors gave him a taste of the mythic. Two men stand out: Edward Turner Carbonell and Captain Neal MacDougal. Although contemporaries, they were, respectively, Milt's grandfather and great-grandfather. Milt liked to characterize Carbonell as an early socialist, who helped set up the Paris commune in 1870 and who eventually got kicked out of England for his politics. There is no evidence for these claims, and later in his life Milt admitted to having "romanticized" Carbonell's political experience. All we know for certain is that Edward was a successful merchant and publisher, who may have been politically enlightened, but was undoubtedly a confirmed capitalist. The Carbonells were originally Huguenots, French Protestants, who were expelled from their homeland in the 1600s and moved to England. The family were merchants and by the time Edward was born in Wales in 1843, the Carbonells were quite well off. Edward spent time in Paris, where he published a newspaper, before moving to the States and finally the Maritimes. Eventually, he wound up in Charlottetown where he edited *The Islander,* a weekly newspaper, and pursued a variety of business interests. It's here that he met his fourth and final wife, Katherine MacDougal, daughter of Captain Neal MacDougal. Milt's great-grandfather MacDougal, another larger-than-life character, was known in the family for generations after his death as "Daddy," and in the poem of that name Milt talks about the man who "seems to start with himself, like Adam":

Daddy didn't drink, smoked sparely,
Didn't save his love, only his money;
Spoke in such clear modulation
He could be heard from poopdeck to prow, from
    masthead to wheel. . . .

MacDougal started out as a ship's carpenter and soon came to be master of his own schooner. In time, he had a small fleet of ships, but lost them all in a storm. By the time Carbonell came and asked him for his daughter's hand, MacDougal was destitute. He struck a bargain with the wealthy merchant: if he could have a place to live and a small income, Carbonell, then near sixty, could marry his sixteen-year-old daughter.

———

When Robert Acorn was twenty-five, he married Katherine and Edward Carbonell's daughter Helen; she was four years younger than him, with bright red hair, an easy laugh, and a strong, stubborn streak. Her hair was her pride and joy, and as a girl, it hung clear to her waist. "They didn't wash Mother's hair in the winter months because it was so long and thick and took a whole day to dry," Mary told me when I interviewed her in the kitchen of the Hooper farmhouse. "They sort of dry-cleaned it with oatmeal and cornstarch. Mother was very proud of her red hair, and she used to tell of being in a Dominion Day Parade representing the sun because her hair was so bright." Helen, however, was not beyond putting principle ahead of her pride. "Dad told her that he wouldn't marry her if she cut her hair, so she cut it," Mary told me. "Of course, the wedding took place anyway, but I always felt that Mother was the one that lost out." Mary said that her father Robert was by all accounts a cheerful and bright child—in later years, her mother would recall him literally rolling in the church aisle, laughing at some forgotten joke until his stomach hurt.

But something happened to poison Robert's outlook: World War I. Before the war, he was a signaler in the Militia. When the war broke out, he signed up and spent a year guarding the Commercial Cable Company's underwater telegraph cable at Hazel Hill, N.S., one of the main communications links between the Old World and the New (and where he undoubtedly ran into a cable company employee by the name of Sidney Bushell, Stan Rogers' maternal grandfather). Eventually, Robert joined the 13th Battalion of the Royal Highlanders. He saw active duty in France, Belgium, and Germany, witnessing first-hand the horror of modern warfare. He was gassed at the third Battle of Vimy, where he saw hundreds of his friends and comrades die on the battlefield. One time, Robert and his platoon took refuge in a great foxhole, and just as one of his men walked in front of him, a shell landed; it blew the man in half, right before Robert's eyes. While Milton's father survived the war without any serious physical injury, the emotional damage was done. "I returned to civilian life a shell-shocked and frightened person," he wrote to his son in 1964. "When I got off the train in Charlottetown I was wishing to God that I could go back to the life I knew. This may all seem melodramatic to you, but I was at that time so filled with suppressed passion and emotions which I didn't understand, and which I considered normal, that I can't recognize myself when I look back to that time. True, I was 'lucky' in not being killed or wounded, but there were no psychiatrists back then, and no one could see my inward hurt." In 1920, he joined Canada Customs and stayed there for thirty-eight years, constantly working to upgrade his standing in the civil service. There were fringe benefits: people could be awfully friendly to a custom's inspector, and as Mary Hooper says, the family "just about swam in molasses." Despite his success in his career, and the respect he held in the community, Robert was not entirely happy in his work; given a preference, he would have preferred to be a priest but, of course, he had a family to feed.

Times were tough on Robert and Helen Acorn. They had five children—Milton, Katherine, Helen, Mary, and Robert. Milton, or Mickey, as they called their oldest, was a sickly child whose monthly drug costs exceeded the family grocery bill. He'd been a robust baby, but all of a sudden his health turned, and he had one infection after another: tonsils, adenoids, sinuses, ears—and then there were the nose-bleeds. The slightest tap or sneeze could set the blood flowing, and more often than not, Helen would have to send for the doctor to come and cauterize poor Mickey's nose. Those were the days before antibiotics, when sunshine was considered the best medicine for whatever ailed you: Mickey Acorn survived, barely, on sunshine, air, water, vitamins, and what little food his mother coaxed him into eating. Mickey Acorn survived because his mother said he would, and she refused to be defeated. Helen was a great organizer who helped keep the family fortunes afloat. Before marriage she had been a top stenographer, and later, after the doctor told her that for the sake of her health she shouldn't do any more housework, she went back to work. That suited Helen fine; she loved working in an office, and had never been fond of housework. To Mickey, his mother was "a goddess of green age," who protected, nursed and nurtured him, a dominating influence who seemed to encompass his entire world. In later years, he fondly remembered "the whole room full" of his mother's smile, with himself "scampering across" its edges.

Because of his illness, Mickey and his mother were constant companions and became extremely close, forging a friendship that he would cherish all his life. His ill health also produced another unexpected benefit; as Milt's other surviving sister Kay Traynor, who lives in Regina explained to me over the phone, the bedridden boy had plenty of opportunity to develop his imagination. "He used to make stories up," Kay said. "He'd take out paper dolls and line them up and have them march around the room, and invent a great battle. He lived in a fantasy world because he was so sick." Mickey missed a lot of school, which was something of a blessing because he had a fierce temper and an odd temperament. Inside the classroom Mickey was disruptive; outside of it, he was bullied and beaten. Still, he showed flashes of intelligence. Despite his poor attendance he never failed a grade, and developed a potent imagination and a quick tongue, what the Irish on The Island called the gift of the gab, a gift that could always bring a smile to his mother's face, and an angry word to his father's lips. As Milt later told Bruce Meyer and Brian O'Riordan, the authors of *In Their Words: Interviews with Fourteen Canadian Writers*, his father was alarmed with his son's overactive imagination. "My dad was a real storyteller," Milt said. "He would talk about his experiences in the war and all of a sudden would wander off in complete fantasy. Yet he was afraid that my imagination would lead me to madness. Of course, you know, it's not true at all. The repression of imagination is what leads to madness."

Despite Milt's ongoing battles with his father, his parents were free thinkers in the Acorn tradition, and encouraged their children to use their heads and express themselves. To some outsiders, the Acorns must have seemed an argumentative lot, but Milt's nephew David Hooper remembers visiting the house as a child and marveling at the level of table talk: "They were an opinionated family, a family that talked about just about everything. Nothing seemed to be taboo. When we used to visit the Acorns, as compared to the rather staid Hoopers, it was interesting. Something was always in the fire. I realize now that it was really free and open as far as intellectual discussions went." Mickey, in particular, reveled in these family discussions, taking particular pride in getting his father's goat; their verbal battles were the stuff of legends in the Acorn household. In the essay "My Life as a Co-adventurer," from *Jackpine Sonnets*, Milt looked back on these battles with a romantic, but ironic, eye:

> My father and I had many bitter quarrels. I'm not referring to mere "you're one—you're another and worse besides" verbal encounters or even spankings, tho both occurred. I'm referring to actual all-out combat. Psychological studies have shown that such a bring-up never really harms the final result—the man; as long as the coercion is consistent. My dad was inconsistent. "Don't dare raise your hand to me!" The key word was *dare*. Tho the old man never seemed to realize that. Up would come my hand and I'd get the proverbial old fertilizer beat out of me. Up 'til I was sixteen or so my father always won. But sometimes I made a good showing. Was my father disappointed? You bet he wasn't. He'd go around boasting for days. In my presence yet! Once, in his presence I had a hot argument with my school principal. Did I get a bawling out for disrespect to my elders? (Besides the fact the principal was right.) No sir, I got congratulations for sticking up for what I thought was right. On the other hand I *did* get many

bawlings out for disrespect to my elders. Small wonder that today my "nerves" are bad (sometimes I live for weeks on tranquilizers and Southern Comfort) by my "nerve" is fantastic.

Oddly, Mickey enjoyed the battles he had with his father, and perhaps it was one area that he felt he could adequately compete. Although short in stature, Robert was extremely strong, and proud of his physical prowess. A scrawny, sickly child, young Mickey felt inadequate in the shadow of this "epitome of masculinity," as he called his father in his unpublished memoir. "Where are all the little men gone? I mean the vital little men with bulging chests and forearms like whipcord. Once, about 1960, I saw one walking down the street, his chest out like a prow, the muscles on his sleeve-rolled-up arms firm with tension, his hands stuck in his pockets. Those were little men who had to prove their equality in a big man's world, do big men's jobs, fight anybody who tried to trample them down. My father was one of them. He could stand on his head right in the middle of the floor, walk on his hands across the room. He proved himself daily, and to me he talked of toughness, of beating down all that challenged me. But I wasn't a man like that. After a few infant years of burgeoning health I caught 'the worms' and the flesh faded off my bones. Nevertheless, my father fed me on his dogma: *Be tough, it's the only way to get along.*"

I wonder, though, if Mickey goaded his father because it gave him a sense of control. While his health was unpredictable—at any moment the dam in his nose might crack, and another river of blood would flow, and Mickey was never sure how teachers and classmates would react to him—he was always certain that, if he pushed the right buttons, Dad would lose his temper. In a funny way, it allowed Mickey to feel heroic, David against Goliath, the tough little man proving himself almost every day. The strategy served its purpose at home. Soon, Mickey would try it out on the complex world that was his Island.

CHAPTER TWO

The Fights

> ... the brain's the target
> and round by round it's whittled
> till nothing's left of a man
> but a jerky bum, humming
> with a gentleness less than human.
> —"The Fights," from *I've Tasted My Blood*

MY SECOND DAY ON THE ISLAND I went on a guided tour of Milt's child-hood haunts. In the morning, I met Mary and her husband Garth Hooper at their farmhouse in Milton, just outside of Charlottetown. The place name was a never-ending source of delight for Mary's brother. "Would you send a taxi out to Milton for Milton?" he'd say every time he called City Cabs, never tiring of the joke. In the last years of his life, when he had returned to P.E.I. to die, Milt spent a lot of his time at the Hooper house, sitting on the lawn, or when it rained, under the big lime tree, jotting notes and poem fragments in his journal, and lecturing at length to anyone foolish enough to enter into a political discussion with him. Milt had a history in the old house, having volun-teered to help build it. "But we had to let him go," Garth told me, with a laugh. "We couldn't afford him! The problem was he'd take so damn long to do a job. He was a perfectionist, which is fine if you're a poet, but not so good when you're a carpenter. Milt really *was* a good carpenter," Mary said, and offered to show me a table that he'd built. If she seemed a little protective, it's because since Milt's death a lot of people had questioned the stories he told, including the one about being a carpenter. This was only my second meeting with Mary, but already I'd made up my mind about one thing: she had adored her older brother. "He had a temper, sure," she told me as we sat at her kitchen table drinking tea, "but he was the kindest man you'd ever meet." After lunch, Mary let me look through a stack of press clippings and family photos. At the very bottom, I came across a copy of *In Love and Anger*, the poetry chapbook Milt self-published in 1956. When I told Mary that a signed *In Love and Anger* in good condition, like this one, was worth $400 or $500 or more, she looked at me trying to figure out, I think, if I was pulling her leg.

Among the photos (Milt with Gwen on their wedding day; Milt with Dief receiving his honourary Ph.D. from the University of P.E.I.) I found an old one of Milt as a child, bunched in the corner of a wicker couch. He couldn't have been more than eight, although even at this stage in his life it was impossible to pin an exact age on him. Mickey was wearing his Sunday best, a wool suit his father had bought him because he thought the suits Aunt Lillie Fairclough sent Mickey were too "sissified," with knee-high socks and ankle-high leather boots. Mickey looked like a cross between a street waif in a silent movie and a drowned rat. He had a big forehead, and large eyes and ears, which took in everything. His eyes were slightly slanted and his cheekbones high; some said Indian blood flowed through his veins. His mouth was small and pinched, and where some children seem blessed with an ever-present smile, Mickey wore a perpetual half-grimace. I'm told his voice was soft and lilting, and when he spoke he'd hesitate and stammer. But he was a cocky bugger who'd go out of his way not just to pick fights, but to pick fights he'd lose. His brother Robert said that on his way to school, Milt would deliberately take a short cut through the Irish neighbourhood where it was a sure bet one of the boys would take a swipe at him. On family outings, it was a given that Mickey would mouth off some bigger kid, luring him into a fight.

When he couldn't lose honestly, he simply stopped trying and let himself get beaten up. Robert recalled one time down by Dead Man's Pond in Victoria Park, when two girls beat Mickey up. "The first girl punched him out, and I can still see him with his leg and arm up for ineffective protection," Robert said, shaking his head in disbelief some fifty years later. "After she was finished, the second girl said, 'Let me have a crack at him.' Milt stood there dutifully while the second girl put on her white gloves so she wouldn't soil her hands with his blood. Then she pounded him, and he just took it." Robert told me this story as we stood on the banks of Dead Man's Pond. He pointed to the exact spot where Mickey had stood to take his licking. I asked Robert how come his brother liked to fight so much, and he just shrugged and smiled and said, "I haven't the slightest idea." Robert was four-and-a-half years younger than his brother, and like Milt lived most of his adult life away from The Island, working for the Maritime Telegraph & Telephone in Nova Scotia. Robert is a writer too—his humorous short articles have appeared in the local papers—and played an important role in Milt's literary development. "I taught him how to scan a poem," Robert says, with some pride. "Milt always thanked me for that."

We wandered for forty minutes through Victoria Park, which offered an interesting contrast to downtown Charlottetown, particularly that area near Confederation Square which has been gentrified and kept in such immaculate shape that you feel like you have to be on your best behaviour. Victoria Park has a more relaxed feel to it, and I got the sense that it hadn't really changed from the days when Helen Acorn would pack a picnic lunch and take her five children down to the park. After our stroll, the five of us—me, Mary, Garth, Robert, and his wife Alta—piled into Robert's car to tour the numerous homes the Acorn children had lived in growing up. They'd moved five or six times (Hillsboro Street, Elm Avenue, Confederation Street, Brighton Road), changing residence as the family fortunes shifted, each house still quite pleasant today, reflecting the moderate middle-class upbringing their parents provided for them. "Milt wrote that he couldn't abide what he was born to," Robert said as we parked in front of one of their childhood homes at 103 North Road, near the park. "Well, among other things he was born to middle-class comforts and middle-class values."

While the other Acorn children seemed to have fond memories of growing up, Milton saw the Charlottetown of his childhood as a hostile place, with new battles ready to break out at every turn, an attitude that was to stay with him the rest of his life. At nine, he tried to be like other kids. He had a paper route, delivering the *Star Weekly* (ten cents a copy, four cents of which was Mickey's); he rode a bike, and even tried skiing, although his parents could only afford the skis—no boots, no poles. But other kids saw Mickey as a sickly outsider, and went out of their way to distance themselves from him. Robert recalled the almost-daily beatings getting so bad that their mother begged their father to buy a pair of boxing gloves and teach Mickey how to protect himself. Nothing changed; Mickey still got into scraps. But he did develop a fascination with the "science" of boxing. He read everything he could about the sport and pored over boxing statistics the same way other Canadian kids studied the scoring records of Howie Morenz, Busher Jackson, and Eddie Shore. At night, Mickey lay awake longing for the day he would step into the ring as a professional boxer, and with every pounding he took, he imagined himself one fight closer to a title shot. As an adult, Milton put on his brave face whenever he spoke of his childhood trials. In "My Life as a Co-adventurer," Milt looks back on rough times with ironic detachment, masking the pain he must have felt:

> As a little lad, dating from about five on, I was quite a fighter. Mind you I didn't say I was a good fighter: in fact I was one of the worst fighters I have ever known. I mean, I was an *enthusiastic* fighter. Size, strength, reputation, didn't bother me in the least. The moment I heard the slightest imputation against my honor (nuances so fine that the average *Irish* chap couldn't detect them) I was there with my fists flying like a dog doing the paddle. I'm not kidding you. That's exactly how I fought in the first place, like a swimmer doing the paddle. (I couldn't swim.) Naturally, especially since I was a sickly child, I took a hell of a beating almost daily. But I wouldn't quit. Had a strong bone structure, flesh like the original superman (I never got a bruise in my life,

unless a bone was actually broken—for instance, I never had a black eye). Didn't need to quit. There was one exception to this. My nose was weak. One whack to the nose and I would bleed like a pig. I wasn't entirely beyond reason. One smack on the nose and I would immediately surrender. On the other hand, I developed sophisticated methods for protecting my nose. Nevertheless I developed no methods for protecting the rest of my body (they didn't need them): and took a terrible series of lickings. I couldn't even beat a boy two years younger than me, if he was stocky. This was because my Dad had told me never to use an uppercut. If you used an uppercut you were liable to break somebody's neck. As if my feeble blows could break anybody's neck. Anybody should know that you can't hit a fighter shorter than you except with an uppercut. This was of the things I didn't know. I told you I was smart, true, but only true in certain ways. Not in fighting. . . . Later in a book (or in the *Toronto Star Weekly*) I read an article on scientific boxing. The chief lesson of that book or article was use your left. I used my left all right. I used my left with such one-sided concentration that I forgot almost entirely about my right. Naturally, all an opponent had to do was to circle around to his left (my right) and pound the piss out of me.

Driving around Charlottetown with the Acorn family, I tried to imagine what life was like for Milt growing up in the midst of the Great Depression. His father always had a paycheque, and while Charlottetown wasn't as hard hit as some of the smaller farm, fishing, and company towns throughout the Maritimes, things were tough. One of Mickey's childhood friends died on the streets from a combination of starvation and exposure, and for the rest of his life Milt was haunted by the image of children begging on every corner. It was an era light years from our own, where oral traditions were still strong, and where the common people were touched by a mood of social unrest.

A man like Cape Breton's Dawn Fraser comes to mind. He was a popular regional poet of the 1920s and 30s whose work I came to know through my wife's uncle Don MacGillivray, a history professor at the University College of Cape Breton. Uncle Don co-edited, with David Frank, a collection of Fraser's writing, *Echoes From Labour's Wars*. Fraser was a curious fellow. He was born near Antigonish in Nova Scotia in 1888. About twelve years later, his family moved to the coal mining boom town of Glace Bay on the northwest tip of Cape Breton. Fraser drifted for several years, working at an odd mix of jobs—nurse, circus barker, grave digger—until the outbreak of World War I. He soon found himself in the army, where, he later recalled "the government became interested in my education and gave me a free course in bayonet fighting." As part of his tour of duty, he was stationed in Siberia for four months, where he took part in an unsuccessful attempt to quash the Russian Revolution. All the while, Fraser was developing his poetic skill, but followed the oral storytelling tradition—in the mode of Robert Service—rather than a literary one. Simply put, his poems were meant to be spoken to an audience of common people. As the introduction to *Echoes From Labour's Wars* explains, Fraser was a kind of modern troubadour:

> He read his verse on the streets, at local union meetings, at parties and at the massive labour and political meetings and the Savoy and Russell Theatres in Glace Bay. His writings appeared in pamphlets, books, magazines and newspapers. For the Glace Bay workers paper, the *Maritime Labour Herald*, he contributed not only stories and verse, but also columns of sports news and advice to the lovelorn. Sometimes his outpourings were simply posted on a bulletin board at the main intersection in Glace Bay. For the workers of industrial Cape Breton, the strong and effective use of language—a sharp tongue or a pointed pun—was one of the weapons at hand. Sharing the principles and prejudices of his community, Fraser was able to articulate common feelings and tell a shared story, and he was an effective and popular presence in the industrial community. . . . Fraser belonged to none of the orthodox schools of poetry in the Maritimes, neither the academic circles around the universities in Halifax and Fredericton, nor the congenial romantics who banded together as the Song Fisher-

men. He was a loner who rarely thought of himself as a literary
man, and tended to regard poetry more as a vice than a vocation.

It's unlikely—but not inconceivable—that Milton Acorn ever heard
Dawn Fraser recite his verses. But there's no doubt that young Mickey
would have come in contact with Fraser's kind of populist troubadour,
and that his own earliest poetic yearnings were influenced not by the
university-anointed literary greats, but by the voices and cadences of
the oral tradition. Certainly the mood of social discontent in the air
during the Depression hung with Milton the rest of his life.

Later, he often claimed that his political awakening occurred at the
ripe old age of eleven, when, as a paperboy, he saw first-hand how the
capitalist system worked, how the downtrodden worker was exploited
by the profit-driven owner. Meanwhile, as he later wrote in the poem
"A Child's Advent in Charlottetown," the local Irish lads earned his
eternal gratitude "for beating respect for the working class" into him.
In an interview on the CBC Television program *Take 30*, Milton elabo-
rated further. "The working class was way on top. If a working class
kid was your friend, he was your friend. There was no doubt about it.
If a middle-class kid was your friend, he was your friend only up to a
certain point. You wanted to watch your back. . . . This is the basis on
my theory of class consciousness." Milton even went so far as to com-
memorate the exact moment he became a socialist. He was looking at
an issue of *True Detective,* according to "My Life as a Co-Adventurer,"
when he noticed the headline on the front page, "Exposed Communist
Plot to Blow Up the Capitol":

> Underneath was portrayed a secret agent (whether Russian or
> American wasn't specified, but I presume he was a Russian) en-
> tering a room full of poison gas, with a gas mask on and firing a
> revolver. I started to form a boy's fantasy on that, putting myself
> firstly in the place of the Americans. But suddenly my eyes went
> back to the word 'CAPITOL.'
>> *This thing of wondrous telling*
>> *I hit the truth by a mistake of spelling*

There was a thing called 'Capitolism.' It had a headquarters called the 'Capitol.' The communists were out to blow up the 'Capitol.' Thus putting an end to 'Capitolism'. . . . In a wink of an eye I was fantasizing from the other end, tho from the Communist side, not the Russian. No sir. I was the heroic Canadian Communist. One of the breed who stormed Vimy Ridge. Who took Teruel and then had it taken back as soon as our backs were turned. I cannot say I never looked back. From then on I looked front and sideways, up and down, back and outside, inside too. Never front and centre. Front and centre is a bourgeois concept. But from that day forward I knew who I was.

CHAPTER THREE

Damnation Machine

All wars have been fought,
and lost,
won,
or just gone by,
and the weapons of the mind
hang in a void.

> —"The Damnation Machine," from
> *I've Tasted My Blood*

ON SEPTEMBER 1, 1939, MICKEY ACORN READ about the Nazi invasion of Poland in the *Charlottetown Patriot*, then got on his bike and rode half a mile to the army recruiting office. It was two days before the official outbreak of World War II: Britain and France would declare war on Germany on September 3, Canada would not follow for another week. Mickey was all of sixteen. Over the previous summer the sickly child had sprouted into a thick-chested six-footer, with an oversized head and hands. He looked five years older than his true age, and the recruiting officer accepted him on the spot. Mickey rushed home to tell his family, but while his father was pleased with his son's patriotic spirit, he wasn't about to let this boy go to war. The elder Acorn used his army connections to get Mickey discharged, then re-enlisted himself. Robert joined the 17th Armoured Reserve Regiment and was soon promoted to Major in Command of the Reconnaissance Squadron. One of the local boys who made his way into Major Acorn's reserve platoon was his future son-in-law, Garth Hooper. "Nobody liked Milt's dad in the reserves," Garth recalled. "He was demanding and tough. Some of the other leaders would loosen up every once in a while and let us have some fun. But not Milt's dad; it was all business with him."

By the age of sixteen Mickey was already flirting with the notion of being a writer, although his first interest was in short stories, not poetry. It made sense to the teenager. Alone in his sick bed for much of his childhood, Mickey had developed a fertile imagination, flights of fancy fueled by his passion for pulp fiction magazines like *Astounding*, *Fantasy & Science Fiction* and *True Detective*. Science fiction appealed to him most of all, perhaps because it was essentially optimistic, the triumph of imagination and intellect over humanity's darker tendencies. This romantic outlook seems to go against the rough and cynical exterior Mickey was developing, but cynicism is often the first refuge of frustrated idealists. He was the kind of person who'd pick up the newspaper to read, with smug satisfaction, stories of cruelty, exploitation and stupidity—his father called it "Milton's daily sneer"—only to be reduced to tears by the report of a child stuck down a well. Mickey's compassionate side was also reflected in the political choices he was making. By the time the war broke out, his boyhood fascination in "Communist Plots" had blossomed into a serious, adolescent interest in political theory, and in particular, the work of Marx, Engels, Lenin, and Stalin. For Milt, this attraction to politics was as natural as eating. "I just had the URGE, URGE, URGE!" he explained in *In Their Words*. "I didn't even bother with sex. My first driving urge was to get into political action."

This drive was enhanced by another natural process: the teenaged Milt was drifting further away from his father and found that his political leanings were a short cut to his father's wrath. All Milt had to do was mention the word "communist" and his father saw red. But like a typical teenager, as Milt strove to distance himself from his father, he also continued to seek his approval. He longed to carry on the family military tradition and prove himself on the battlefield. On his eighteenth birthday he told his parents he wanted to enlist. His mother hesitated, but his father told Milt that he was old enough to make up his own mind. With that obstacle out of the way, Milt still had political concerns. He worshiped Stalin and the Soviet communists, but on August 22, 1939, Uncle Joe had suddenly, and to the surprise of many of his comrades within the Communist International, signed a non-aggression pact with Germany. On the home front, the Canadian government openly suppressed the Communist Party, and interned thousands of Canadians as political prisoners under the Defense of Canada Act. However, all Milt's ambiguity evaporated on June 22, 1941, when Hitler turned on his ally and launched an assault on the Soviet Union. The very next day, Milt walked down to the recruiting office and signed on for the second time.

Not everyone shared Milt's enthusiasm for the war, and many people on the left were disgusted with the apparent proof that capitalism had yet to learn its lesson. One such left-wing critic was Dorothy Livesay, who was a student at the University of Toronto at the outbreak of the war, and who would later become the poet Milt modelled his own career after. ("It was Dorothy who made me envious, made me want to be a poet," Milt told *The Western Voice* in March 1974.) Livesay was born in Winnipeg in 1909 to a very literate family; both her parents were journalists, and her mother Florence Randal Livesay also had a reputation as a poet. From an early age, Livesay was an independent spirit, an early feminist and active socialist, and at one time was an avowed Communist. Directly before the war she was studying at the Sorbonne in Paris; she returned to Canada to find "a strong working-class movement of the youth against fascism and the war," a movement that soon filtered into the artistic community. In a special 1979 edition of the feminist arts journal *Room of One's Own*, Dorothy Livesay recalls this now-forgotten opposition. "There was nothing outrageous about this: all leading writers and artists in the world were involved," Livesay said. "Canadian poets like A.M. Klein, Leo Kennedy, and Frank Scott were in the thick of it. But Canadians today, even those who lived through it, don't seem to realize that we were part of a world movement which was trying to help avoid war, the culmination of which was the Spanish Civil War, in which 1,200 Canadians, mostly unemployed, fought for the Republic. Only 600 of them came back alive." After the war, Livesay emerged as one of the country's major "social realist" poets who strove to bring a new relevance and vitality to Canadian poetry. She lives today in a Victoria nursing home, largely neglected by the literary community.

––––––––

Army life suited Milton Acorn. It was, according to his sister Kay, "a rough life, and there were a lot of people who were rough like he was." Shortly after enlisting, Milton was put on a troop train and shipped to Camp Borden, a military training centre north of Toronto. The trip must have been stressful for Milton; he'd never been away from home before, and lacked a lot of basic social skills. Six weeks later, he was on the move again, on the train back to the east coast where a troop ship was waiting to take him and the other recruits to the killing fields of Europe. The ship was the *Cameronian*, part of an allied convoy taking fresh troops and supplies to Britain. It was a confusing moment for young Milt as he crossed the *Cameronian*'s gangway. He was finally getting the chance to prove himself in battle, to be a war hero like his father and grandfather. But as young and immortal as he was, he must have felt a twinge of fear. The war was not going well. The Nazis were advancing on several fronts, their air raids on London continued relentlessly, and meanwhile, German U-boats were on constant watch for allied ships, posing a real threat to the *Cameronian*'s safety.

Half-way across the Atlantic, Milton's worst fears were realized. The convoy encountered a pack of German U-boats, and the two sides engaged in an agonizing game of cat and mouse. As he recalled in *In Their Words*, a depth charge dropped by one of the allied ships changed the course of his life. "It was a blast, just a pure blast," Milt said. "I didn't have enough sense to cover my ears. Typical story of the young intellectual. I should have been an officer, but they made me a sergeant instead and there was no one behind me to say 'Put your hands over your ears.' I looked at the depth charge and said to myself: 'The blast from that charge is going to reach me in nineteen seconds,' so I started counting but never thought to put my hands over my ears. . . . It was a near-death experience. There's lots of things I'm terribly afraid of now, but not death."

The blast knocked Milton out for a few minutes, but otherwise he seemed fine until two days later when he was struck with a terrible earache. He was taken off the *Cameronian* on a stretcher and immediately shipped to a hospital in Britain. Doctors performed a mastoid operation, which left a large scar on his face just where the jawbone and neck meet. A little while later, German planes bombed the hospital and the army moved him to a solarium in Scotland. The operation put an end to the chronic ear infections that had troubled Milton since childhood, and while his physical problems seemed under control, the combined stress of two bomb attacks and his serious medical problem had a profound emotional effect on him. "It drove me completely cuckoo," he said. "I refused to die though. I even fought to rally myself and get back in the active service." But his efforts were wasted. The army, which always has a hard time dealing with the psychological effects of warfare, kept Milton under medical observation for a year as they tried to figure out what to do with him. Finally, he gave them an ultimatum: "Send me to active service, or send me home." On January 11, 1943, doctors discharged Milton and shipped him home.

On his return to Charlottetown, Milton was duly honoured for his military service, receiving the Defense Medal, the Canadian Volunteer Services Medal with Clasp, and, a few years later, the War Medal 1939-45. But the man who came home that winter was very different from the boy who'd left a year and a half earlier. For starters, the mastoid operation left him nearly deaf, and it took several years for his hearing to fully recover. But what struck the family most was his emotional decline. Kay recalls that he was "very paranoid," and was convinced that government officials and others were watching his every move. He also suffered from chronic depression, talked openly of suicide, and like many veterans, turned to alcohol for relief. "It was a very hard and embarrassing time," Milt confessed to his interviewers in 1984. Perhaps what troubled him most was that he felt like a coward, or at the very least, felt as if he hadn't lived up to the standard set by his father. Growing up, he'd been fascinated by heroism, with physical and mental toughness, and as an adult he became obsessed with his personal epic mythology. But when he got the chance to test himself in battle, Milt literally "lost his nerve." It was a blow to his own rigid perception of what it meant to be a man. And once again, he was locked in a kind of competition with his father. He never even saw active duty, yet he came home even more emotionally scarred by war than his father had been, and for the rest of his life, Milt seemed haunted by memories of war. The poet David McFadden recalls driving with Acorn in the early seventies when suddenly a fierce hailstorm hit. As the hail battered the car's roof, Milt threw his hands over his head and dove to the floor screaming, an apparent flashback to the naval battle he witnessed on the deck of the *Cameronian*.

The years following his discharge were tough on Milt. He wanted to leave Charlottetown, to strike out on his own and make a name for himself—exactly how, he wasn't sure—but something held him back. His mental and physical health were poor, although the mastoid operation had helped his ear problems, and his hearing was slowly returning. But Milt made the best of his situation. There are some reports that he dropped out of school in Grade Six, but his family remembers an earnest student who eventually completed Grade Ten. Like a lot of young men, particularly in those postwar years, Milt was unsure of his future. He knew he had a creative talent burning inside, but he had little idea how to stoke this talent, and was certain he could never use it to make a living. More and more, he talked of being a writer. He was always working on a new short story, and was even sending some out to magazines. He was also becoming more interested in poetry, and somewhere along the line he came across *A New Anthology of Modern Poetry*. In unpublished notes, Milton wrote he had "the usual philistine prejudices against poetry," but this anthology, with its emphasis on "poetry as direct speech about real problems," converted him. Undoubtedly, Milton was referring to a book edited by the American poet Selden Rodman, published in 1938. This anthology was a landmark statement of the modernist movement in poetry, and I can easily see how young Milt became enthralled by it; Rodman's intelligent and eclectic choices—Lewis Carroll's "Jabberwocky" and W.C. Handy's

"St. Louis Blues" taking their place along side Housman, Yeats, Sand-
burg, Pound, cummings, Auden, Eliot, and sixty-three others—are as
fresh today as they were fifty years ago. With this collection, Rodman
deliberately set out to overcome what he saw as a block to the popular
acceptance of modern poetry—the belief on the part of anthologists
that it must be Highly Serious, and therefore Highly Dull. "People
who dislike the very idea of poetry," Rodman writes, "dislike it as they
dislike over-earnest people. . . . Poetry is no better and no worse than
human nature; it is profound and shallow, sophisticated and naïve, dull
and witty, bawdy and chaste in turn."

What exactly is "modern" poetry? Critics continue to debate the
definition of the term, and even its existence, but I think of modernism
as a literary movement by default, a reaction against the conventions
that poets had come to associate with the Romantic tradition, particu-
larly conventions of form, such as regular rhythm and rhyme patterns,
and a tendency toward themes of myth and heroism. The popular
belief is that the Romantic poets preceded the modernist ones, but it's
not simply a question of chronology. While the first part of this century
leading up to World War II can be thought of as the Golden Age of
Modernism, the literary values important to this movement can be
found throughout history. "Whitman and Dickinson are modern to be
sure," writes Rodman in his introduction to *A New Anthology of Mod-
ern Poetry*, "but so are Blake and Marvell and Donne. The demarcation
of modernity is a personal matter at best." While he resists defining the
term, Rodman offers as a guide this list of the "characteristics of mod-
ernity": the use of imagery based on everyday speech; the lack of con-
ventions of form or "poetic" language; a disregard of conventional,
cause-and-effect logic; an interest in the common man as opposed to
the hero; and a focus on social realities rather than ideals of heaven or
nature. In effect, Rodman's vision of modernism was an attempt to
wrestle poetry from the faceless literary elite—the "priesthood," he
called it—and back to the people. I can imagine a shudder run up
Milt's spine as he read Rodman's call to action:

> In a sensuous world ever-present and ever-beautiful, it is the
> sensitive poet who should affirm the fact so sharply that we are

called upon to live vividly ourselves. He will affirm the good in the very teeth of man's inhumanity to man, without minimizing the corrupt. A painter must get along with his eyes, a sculptor with his touch, a musician with his ear; but a poet must add to each one of these perceptions *intellect*. . . . If anybody should be above the battle, it is the poet. If anybody should be *in* the battle, it is he. He alone must take sides and still reserve half his sympathy for the enemy. His heart must be involved, but his mind clear as spring water. Nothing can be too ugly, too sordid, too brutal, too immediate, too mean to evoke the poet's interest. Yet his own sensibilities must be incorruptible; he must be virtuous, if not chaste; devout without subscribing to creeds; humble, but not pious.

A failure in the art of war, Acorn was understandably drawn in by the revolutionary possibilities of this "modern" poetry. He was an idealistic young man, not particularly handsome, so poetry offered him a chance to garner a young woman's attention. Poetry also suited his personality. He wasn't a "linear thinker"; in conversation, he'd go off on tangents, as one topic reminded him of another. As a poet, he could use this sensitivity to connections to his advantage. Some of Acorn's earliest poetic efforts survive. They are vague and awkward, and full of the obscure philosophizing that young writers confuse with art. Still, there is a hint of things to come. In 1945, he wrote "A Chill Poem," his oldest surviving work which already holds some of the elements—the lonely mysticism, the totemic fascination with nature—that would later become Acorn trademarks:

If I, on a lonely road,
Meet a demon in the night,
His wild eyes gleaming hungrily . . .

Writing wasn't Milton's only artistic interest, for he was also drawn to the theatre. He came from a family of "hams," as his sister Kay put it; being on stage helped satisfy his deep need to be noticed and appreciated, and once he memorized all his lines, he could speak in public without his usual stammer. He started acting in the Anglican Young People's Association, one of the best amateur theatre groups in the province. His first role was as Sganarelle in *Who Stole the Bishop's Candlesticks?*, which was directed by Stuart Dickson, the local news announcer. The show won top honours at the provincial drama festival, and Milt was named Best Actor ("Milton Acorn gives a splendid performance as the rascally old Sganarelle," a local theatre critic wrote). Later, Milt moved on to the Charlottetown Little Theatre Guild. Peter Shama of Charlottetown was Milt's neighbour, and the two appeared in several plays together. Shama says that Milt took acting seriously and got quite good at it. "We did a lot of plays, and a lot of sketches too, a lot of off-the-cuff sketches that we'd just dream up," Shama recalls. "The hall was usually packed. We were the cat's meow there for a while."

While Milt dabbled in the youthful pursuits of poetry and the theatre, he tried to get down to the serious adult matter of finding a career. His first job after his discharge was at the Provincial Hospital—the same hospital where Milt had been born—which had been converted to a home for chronic care patients. Milt was a good worker, but found it hard to leave the job behind at the end of the day. Mary remembers her brother's frustration with how the patients just sat around, looking out the windows. "So he gathered a bunch of knitting needles," Mary says. "He got the old ladies knitting, and organized games for kids. The patients really liked Milt. He seemed to understand what they were going through and did what he could to make their lives a little more pleasant."

For his first attempt at a career, Milt followed in his father's footsteps and joined the civil service. To prepare, he took a business course, then in 1946 wrote the civil service exams, which he passed with flying colours. He applied for several jobs and finally landed one in Moncton, New Brunswick as a clerk in the Unemployment Insurance Commission. He stayed on for almost a year—spending most of his time agitating for a union—and quit after coming to the simple realization that the nine-to-five grind wasn't for him. Milt moved back to The Island and looked for work. He took a carpentry course sponsored by the Department of Veterans' Affairs, and at night picked up extra cash working on the docks. After completing his training, Milt worked as a carpenter with his uncle, Stanley Bryant. Bryant was lanky, good-natured and even-tempered, a man that Milt would later honour in a simple lyric, "The Retired Carpenter":

> Tools, grips sweat-polished
> in a dinted box, loose
> at all angles,
> half of them vanished. . . .

Politics also took its toll on Milt's carpentry career. As he said in *In Their Words*, communism became his over-riding obsession: "I had been in the Canadian army, fighting against the same enemy Joseph Stalin was fighting against. Just after that there was a lot of anti-Stalin propaganda, and, I thought, there must be something to this or they wouldn't be putting on such a show against him. All the time I was taking my carpentry course I couldn't do anything right because my mind was always thinking, always thinking, saying 'communism is right, communism is right.' There was a strike on in the town, then, and it was odd how many of my mates just couldn't get the political implications. They were all for the workers, of course, but when it came to a vote they voted for the man who broke the strike." In any case, Milton wasn't long for The Island. By now, he was burning to be a writer, and knew that if he wanted to make a name for himself he had to leave his home. But where to go? And how could he afford to live? And why go anyway? What was the chance that he would make it as a writer when thousands of others failed? At times like this, when he most needed to make a decision, his "damned worrying neuroses," the after-effect of his traumatic war experiences, left Milt paralyzed with uncertainty.

CHAPTER FOUR

El Cortijo

> ... if you must remember me
> Let this poem be the memory;
> For at *El Cortijo* I learned to look like a rock ...
> —"Homage to El Cortijo," unpublished

Montreal, circa 1953

EL CORTIJO WAS UNUSUALLY BUSY for a Thursday night. McGill University was only seven blocks away from the coffee shop, and judging by the number of students packed around the tiny tables, sipping coffee and talking an endless din, Milton Acorn reckoned the winter semester had just ended. Milt put his pen down for a moment. Nearby, two elderly men played chess in absolute silence, their eyes never leaving the board. At the back of the room, a teenaged girl softly played a Chopin étude on the old upright piano as a boy beside her hammered the table with his fist, arguing wildly with two of his friends. Milt picked up his pen and began to write:

> *(The scene: a country fair)*
> A merry-go-round hangs music on the air
> That bubbles like a live electric brook,

It's all unseen
This is the track
With all the midway's joys behind the back
Of filling stands, serene, white-washed and worn.
And on the track, intent upon their business
Stern drivers put the racers through their paces.

Milt read the lines, then reread them, shaking his head. Too forced.
Too old-fashioned. He scratched them out and tried to concentrate.
Milt cut an odd figure; spread over the table like dinner, his nose in a
book or his pen scribbling fiercely on a napkin, emerging every once in
a while—like a whale surfacing for air—to sip his coffee and scan the
room with his intense, bug-like eyes. He liked to write at El Cortijo.
The coffee shop was in the heart of Montreal, on Clark Street one
block west of St. Lawrence Boulevard. It was clean, much cleaner than
his room at 4553 Notre Dame East, which was waist-deep in papers,
books and dirty clothes; he always intended to clean it up, but never got
around to it. That was the east side of Montreal, a low-rent, working
class neighbourhood, light years away from the literary community
that congregated near McGill. And El Cortijo was warmer too. When
that north wind howled, it rattled through the window seams, as Milt
tugged the blanket over his head and cursed in the sincere belief that it
was colder in his little room than it was outside on the street. Most of
all, Milt liked El Cortijo for the companionship. Although it was a big
city—much bigger than Charlottetown—Milt found that Montreal
could be frightfully lonely. He'd arrived there late in 1949 at the re-
quest of the Department of Veterans' Affairs, who'd dispatched him to
the military hospital at St. Anne de Bellevue for "observation." The
plain truth was that the army didn't know what to do with Milt; the
war had left his nerves in such bad shape he couldn't hold down a job.
On Uncle Stanley Bryant's advice, Milt had applied for a disability
pension in Charlottetown. At St. Anne de Bellevue the doctors quickly
identified Milt as a chronic depressive, and offered him a lobotomy,
which he kindly declined. They kept Milt under observation for a few
months, then released him, having yet to make a decision on his dis-
ability pension. Set free in Montreal, Milt lived off his small veteran's

pension, unemployment insurance, and the little money his mother
managed to send him. This financial dependence took its toll on his
already low self-image; Milt came from a world where a man earned
his keep and made his own way in the world.

For a while, his mental state was so tenuous that his mother moved
to Montreal, got a job with Royal Trust, and took care of her son. But
at El Cortijo, Milt could leave his troubles behind. The name literally
meant "the cut man," the Spanish term for jellyfish, an image his
poetic imagination appreciated; like Milt, the jellyfish was a detached
brain with no corporeal connections, alone and adrift yet with a sense
of purpose. At El Cortijo, Milt was *the cut man,* part of the crowd yet
separate, silent in the ocean of white noise. He had a strong sense of
destiny, yet he wasn't exactly sure what that destiny was to be. The
glory of proletariat socialism burned inside him, and at times he sus-
pected that fate was calling him to be a great revolutionary leader; just
as he used to lie awake at night imagining himself Joe Louis or Max
Schmelling, he now imagined himself another Lenin leading his peo-
ple out of the capitalist wilderness and into communism's promised
land.

Or maybe a writer's life was in the cards for him. He had talent to
burn—his mother had seen it years ago, and encouraged him at every
step—but even in this simple decision he was torn between writing the
science fiction which enthralled his imagination or the poetry which
took him to the darkest reaches of his own heart. Right now, he was
working on a trail-blazing piece called "Grey Girl's Gallop," in which
he combined both his literary interests into one form, a kind of short
story in verse. He'd already sent an earlier draft to Margaret Fairley,
editor of the Toronto-based magazine *New Frontiers*. Fairley re-
sponded right away. The poem needed work but had potential, and
she hoped that Milt would take another crack at it.

Milt looked at the lines he'd just erased. On second thought, they
weren't that bad. It was somewhat in the outdated Romantic tradition,
but that never hurt; even the best editors were twenty years behind the
times. Milt bit his lip, and submerged again into the ocean of his
imagination. In no time at all, he'd completely rewritten the poem. He
lifted his eyes and realized that the coffee shop was almost empty now;

in the corner, a heavyset French Canadian swept up, as the waitress eyed Milt hopefully. Taking the hint, Milt packed up his journals and papers, and left the warmth of El Cortijo behind in the cold night air.

———

While Milton's move to Montreal was triggered by his medical and emotional problems, he couldn't have picked a better spot. The city was the most progressive, cosmopolitan place in the country, and its writers and poets had been on the leading edge of Canadian Literature for thirty years. In particular, Montreal was the hotbed for the Canadian modernist movement. While earlier in this century, individual poets like Arthur Stringer, F.O. Call, and Raymond Knister were exploring this new wave of poetry, there was no organized movement, and as Susan Gingell writes in *The Oxford Companion to Canadian Literature*, the dominant voices in Canadian poetry "were still heavily influenced by the choice of subject matter and the spirit, verse forms, and diction of English Romantic and Victorian poetry."

Bliss Carman was the best-known and perhaps most talented of the Canadian Romantics. Born in Fredericton, New Brunswick in 1861, Carman was a distant relative of Ralph Waldo Emerson, and was strongly influenced by the mysticism which coloured the work of the American romantics. For a while, he was associated with the group known as the Song Fishermen, named after the leftist Halifax literary magazine that published their work. Other poets in this group included Charles G.D. Roberts, Kenneth Leslie, and Joe Wallace. Carman believed that the spiritual and natural worlds were interrelated, and his poems often used descriptions of nature as a springboard to meditations on the nature of man. Like other Romantics, Carman saw his art as an antidote to the scientific rationalism that dominated thought at the turn of the century. In his 1903 essay "Subconscious Art," which appeared in *The Kinship of Nature*, Carman summarized his aim as a poet:

> ... I should not merely wish to set down my conclusions about life and the universe; I could accomplish that better by being a

trained philosopher. I should not merely want to convey to you new and important facts about nature; I could do that better by being a scientist. I should not want to convince your mind only, for I could do that better by logic and rhetoric. But I should wish to do all these things and win your sympathy as well. I should not only wish to make you believe what I say, but believe it passion- ately—with your whole heart. In order to do this I should have to secure free communication of spirit, as well as of mind. I should not only have to satisfy reason, I should have to lull and charm it. I should have to hypnotize that good warder of your house before he would allow me to enter. Just as I had to mesmerize myself with the cadence of my lines before I could fully make them express my whole nature, so you in your turn as reader would have to feel their undefinable magic before you could appreciate and enjoy my poems to the utmost capacity of your nature. I could only secure this result through the senses, through the mo- notonous music of my verse.

While the Romantic voice dominated post-Confederation literature, it wasn't the only voice to be heard. Archibald Lampman was a nine- teenth-century Canadian poet whom Acorn would later cite as a direct inspiration. Lampman was born in 1861 in a small community in what was then known as Canada West, and now known as Ontario. After an unsuccessful stab at teaching, Lampman got a job at the post office in Ottawa where he worked for sixteen years, never rising above the position of postal clerk, second class. In 1887, he married a woman who had enough money to allow him to self-publish his first collection of verse, *Among the Millet and Other Poems*. Two more titles were publish- ed during his short lifetime, along with numerous essays and commen- taries, many of which openly explored socialism. In 1889, Lampman fell for a fellow postal clerk named Katherine Waddell, and the two lived together for some time. He died in obscurity in 1899, leaving behind the legacy of a man whose lifestyle, politics, and poetry were light years ahead of their time.

It wasn't until 1925 that the modernists found a clear voice in this country. That was the year that poets F.R. Scott and A.J.M. Smith helped found *The McGill Fortnightly Review*, a student magazine out of Montreal's McGill University which became the focal point of the movement. While the members of this "McGill Movement" aligned themselves with their contemporaries in Britain and America, essentially following Selden Rodman's "characteristics of modernity" and striving, in Smith's words, to create a "new poetry" that "spoke to people in their own language," they added some uniquely Canadian elements. Typically, the issue of "national identity" came into play, with the new wave of poets and critics looking back on their literary heritage and finding, as Douglas Bush put it in an essay in the December 1926 *Canadian Forum*, a nation "trying desperately to be literary." The booster-club mentality had left Canada with a woeful legacy that included "bulky histories of Canadian literature, appraising the product of every citizen who ever held a pen; bulky anthologies preserving almost everything metrical that has sprung from the Canadian brain; little books celebrating the genius of people who in another country would not get beyond the poetry corner of the local newspaper; reprints of Canadian "classics" which not even antiquity can render tolerable."

Over time, Frank Scott emerged as a leader of the original McGill Movement. Scott was a remarkable man in his own right, distinguished in literature, law and politics. He was born in Quebec City in 1899. His father was Frederick George Scott, himself a respected poet and theologian. For most of his adult life, Frank Scott both taught and practiced law, and, like a lot of thoughtful people who'd witnessed first-hand the devastation of the Depression, he was active in left-wing politics. He helped establish the League for Social Reconstruction, and was one of the early presidents of the Cooperative Commonwealth Federation, precursor to the New Democrat Party. In his spare time, he wrote numerous volumes of poetry in a style that was sometimes satirical, often elegant, but always deliberately modern.

While this first wave of modernism was an important step in Canadian literature, it wasn't until the 1940s, as the new poetry fused with an emerging social consciousness, that Canadian modernism began to find a distinctive voice. With their outlook tainted by two World Wars, poets were no longer content to ruminate on nature and art; they strove for "social realism" by looking at the world with all its problems and imperfections; truth was no longer an ideal to be obtained, it was the fact of human existence, to be at least observed, if not experienced. With this change in content came a gradual change in form.

Rather than the regular rhymes and rhythms that characterized Romantic poetry, and overlapped into the McGill Movement, the post-war modernists were interested in "free verse," a much more open-ended poetic structure that aimed to reflect the patterns of everyday speech. With varying line lengths, and no set metres, poets saw free verse as a more natural way of writing. It wasn't a new form; passages of the King James' version of the Bible use free verse—"The Song of Songs" for instance—and it was a popular form among French, English, and American poets in the nineteenth century, including Walt Whitman, who used free verse in his influential *Leaves of Grass*.

By the 1950s, McGill University had become the centre of a new wave of modernist poets, including Louis Dudek, Irving Layton, Patrick Anderson and later, Leonard Cohen, and added a Toronto connection through Raymond Souster and his Contact Press. The new modernists took their poetical and political lead from Frank Scott. Most of them leaned left, regarding both the Depression and World War II as proof of the fallibility of capitalism; however, the new modernists turned to the heart of the capitalist world for guidance.

American poets like Ezra Pound and William Carlos Williams were important figures, as was Charles Olson, although he was more influential for his critical writing than for his other literary work. Olson was a literary giant, literally, standing six foot eight or nine. He was born in Massachusetts in 1910, and studied at Harvard and Yale before accepting a teaching position at the Black Mountain College in North Carolina. Olson's *The Maximus Poems* was a landmark in modern poetry, while his 1959 essay "Projective Verse" was an essential statement of the American modernist movement and created the critical framework for postmodernism in that country. Olson was against the "print bred" non-projective verse, the dominant poetic form of the age "despite the work of Pound and Williams," and favoured "projective verse" which was based on "certain laws and possibilities of the breath." Olson's point was that poems had evolved from a spoken to a written medium, and in the process, the line had become the basic unit of poetry. He advocated a return to poetry based on breath and sound patterns, a process which would ultimately affect the kind of poetic forms because, Olson believed, form was an extension of content. In the end, Olson wasn't advocating a return to the oral tradition, but rather the development of a new kind of poetic thought, a poetics based on the intricacies of breath and cadence.

Canadian poets in the 1950s were less interested in a revolution of form than in social reform, and took it upon themselves to shatter the last vestiges of Canadian Romanticism. Poet and professor Louis Dudek was one of the most influential members of this second wave of modernists. Although he's now approaching his eighties, he remains an active writer and literary critic. When I spoke to him, he modestly recalled his efforts in the 1950s. "We knew that we were affecting Canadian poetry as a whole, because we knew it was quite possible to do," Dudek told me. "The modern replacing the nineteenth century in Canada was inevitable. It wasn't our doing; it was something that was inevitable. Anyone who began it would have been given credit for it. And you have to remember that the group was small. It's not like today where there are scores, even hundreds, of poets around. We were a concentrated group, a community that was aware of its own value." Dudek says that the modernist movement in Canada did not occur in a vacuum; French Canadian poets were also moving away from the Romantic tradition, but it took French writers a little longer to make the break. "The French poets had the same kind of problem, even more extreme, and they broke out of it very slowly. It was only in the mid-fifties when the Quiet Revolution began that the breakthrough began to happen."

There were also parallels in the U.S., where Beat writers like Allen Ginsberg and Jack Kerouac (who was of French-Canadian descent) were making a mark with their loosely structured, emotionally charged work. The language and imagery were often explicit, and while it shocked some, it was typically American, as much an experiment in democracy as it was a literary movement. Dudek says that while there were similarities between the Canadian Modernists and the Beats—both movements represented rebellion and liberation for their cultures—there were also essential differences. "We had more sense of structure then they had; they would just get up on the platform and rant. For the Beats it was an exercise in personal expression, but I think we always kept the broader social picture in mind."

It was against this backdrop of artistic revolution tempered with a social conscience that Milton Acorn studied the craft of poetry. He immersed himself in the literary and left-wing underground of the time, joining writing and political workshops where he struggled to find an identity that would unify both his interests. His guide into this world was Louise Harvey, who was at times Milt's landlord, and an intimate friend. Harvey was an interesting character. Her first husband had been a prominent lawyer, and she had been a radical and a poet, and frequently opened her home on Summerville Street in Montreal's fashionable Westmount area to literary and communist discussion groups. Melany Cleveland is Louise Harvey's daughter, and lives in Vermont. When I spoke to her by phone, she recalled Milt from her childhood. "He was quite a physical character," she said. "I remember he had hefty, hefty features. He wasn't the kind who played with us kids a lot. He was quiet, and bearlike." Cleveland also remembered a dramatic incident in her home. In the middle of the night, she was awakened by Milt hollering and banging on the bedroom door. The house was on fire. Milt led the girl, her two brothers and her mother through the smoke. "He smashed a hole through the kitchen window, and we all went from one house to the next."

Louise Harvey was also the one who introduced Milt to Margaret Fairley's *New Frontiers*, and encouraged him to submit "Grey Girl's Gallop." The magazine published the poem in its Winter 1953 edition. Credited to "A," who was identified only as a "Prince Edward Island worker," it was the first time Milt's work appeared in print. He started the poem after a visit to the race track; eventually it became a 250-line political allegory, about a harness racehorse who longs to free herself from the confines of a trot:

"Oh for a gallop, one good gallop!
Just let me hit the ground with a wallop!

Just to release my inhibitions!
To hell with trotting and its traditions! . . .

Finally, unable to restrain herself anymore, Grey Girl breaks into a glorious gallop, "Not the prim pretty gait of civilization/But a passionate rout—pure barbarization!" Grey Girl represented the unbridled spirit of the working classes; the track owner, the forces of capitalism that had set out to harness and regulate the lives of the common man. The politics were heavy-handed, the poem itself rough and rather old-fashioned, in many ways closer to the oral tradition-style of poetry of men like Dawn Fraser and Joe Wallace—the latter was directly involved with *New Frontiers*—than to any particular literary movement. However, there was a genuine energy to "Grey Girl's Gallop," and an attention to detail and craft that suggested that this immature writer had a certain intelligence and literary imagination:

> I'll just be old-fashioned
> And end with a moral. You will note the impassioned
> Gallop of Grey Girl had no special purpose
> But only to do it and use up her surplus
> Of joy, which once spurned cannot be collected.
> As for those who did things because they expected
> To harvest a profit of money or glory—
> Well, whether they managed isn't the story:
> But Grey Girl was sure from the moment she started
> To get what she asked for. When life was imparted
> To men and to horses both races knew this
> "A thing is well done which is done for its own bliss
> Or else done for life—living now or begotten."
> Most horses remember:
> Most men have forgotten.

Milt, who was now thirty, was understandably elated with his first publication. He wrote to his sister Mary to deliver the good news, while complaining that no one really understood this "trail-blazing" piece. "They try to judge it by the standards of what has gone before and generally miss the point," Milt wrote. "My 'Grey Girl's Gallop' was read, enjoyed, but I haven't met a single person who understood it. But you see in this case, it was a work so overpowering, so full of striking observations, that they printed it anyways."

It's doubtful, though, that someone as astute as Margaret Fairley missed the point of the poem. Fairley was a writer and social commentator herself, and wife of painter-poet-professor Barker Fairley, an early champion of the Group of Seven, and the man who suggested in 1920 that the University of Toronto radical undergraduate paper *The Rebel* go national under a new title, *The Canadian Forum*. The first edition of *New Frontiers* hit the newsstands in February 1952, offering Canadians an eclectic, radical, pro-worker, and anti-capitalist view of the world. Despite its serious political side, *New Frontiers* reverberated with optimism and hope. Margaret Fairley's opening comments in the first issue set the tone for what was to come:

> *New Frontiers* aims to give Canadian people a true and passionate picture of their own character and destiny. We will publish stories, poems, songs, pictures and critical, historical and scientific articles revealing the Canadian and world significance of the aspirations of our people towards a genuine democracy in which alone they can find a free, peaceful and plentiful life. *New Frontiers* will encourage our artists and writers to turn to the real lives and hopes, past and present, of the Canadian people. Young writers and artists, determined not to sell their souls, will, it is hoped, find an outlet here. Without peace and independence Canada and her arts cannot prosper. In a variety of living forms *New Frontiers* will bring its readers a picture of the world-wide movement for peace and of Canada's vital place in this picture. . . . This culture cannot thrive if it is choked by the flood of the cynical, degenerate products of U.S. commercialism, anymore than the people can prosper if their country is mined of its goods and money by being turned into a pit for U.S. investors. *New Frontiers* will expose the danger to the Canadian people of the war-foster-

ing U.S. culture, while strengthening its ties with the democratic culture of the American people. We will build a consciousness of our own Canadian cultural achievements and seek to develop and enrich them.

As I read copies of *New Frontiers* at the University of Victoria library, I got a sense of Milton's political environment. As much as *New Frontiers* was a "communist" magazine, it was more a humanist voice, placing the rights and dignity of individuals above any specific party directive, and a particular importance on the role of the arts played in enriching the everyday world. In the issue in which "A," the anonymous Prince Edward Island worker, first appeared, there were also articles by Jean-Paul Sartre on "Peace: The Reality of Life," Sergei Prokofiev on "The Purpose of Music," along with a number of wonderful wood cuts by several different artists, an impassioned plea for the lives of Ethel and Julius Rosenberg, short stories and poems, including "Such Guests to Guard" by Joe Wallace, the most famous labour poet in the country. In a way, the magazine was a manual for Milton's intellectual development. He was inspired to read widely in philosophy, politics, science and the arts, in search of context and content for the literary fire which burned within him.

CHAPTER FIVE

In Love and Anger

> "X" is a moderate politician
> He's for moderate injustice,
> moderate unemployment,
> moderate inequality.
> He's against war
> but only moderately.
> —Untitled, unpublished

IN JUNE OF 1953, Milton attended the Montreal Congress for Expression of Opinions on Peace, a socialist forum. Although he was painfully shy, Milt decided to give a short talk to the 300 delegates. He wrote a four-page speech, then discarded all but one page and nervously took the podium. His subject was "The Problems of the Writer in The Cold War Era"; he talked of the modernist's struggle for "realism," and although he fell short of publicly declaring himself a communist—that could reduce his chance of getting a disability pension, he feared—he pledged his allegiance to the working classes and denounced the vast majority of writers who squandered their art writing about the "rich and criminal minority." Milt was stunned by the response; he was interrupted several times by applause, and afterwards people came up to him, offered their congratulations and asked where his writing could be found.

For a struggling poet, this first moment of public recognition was electric. "It made me more anxious to achieve realism," Milt wrote to his sister Mary. "Tho I continue as before, to find my own way to it. My definition of realism is broader than yours, it corresponds with the Soviet definition which includes 'All that which reflects truly on the world and points to a joyous future for Mankind.'" Milt finished this letter on a note of almost manic elation. "As a matter of fact I do want to be Shakespeare," he wrote. "The times are ripe for one—never before or since Shakespeare's days, and never before or since the days of Homer, have such new vistas of truth been opened and waited for the artists' penetration. I myself may not possess the capacities of a Shakespeare within myself, but it's certain that if enough young writers try, a Shakespeare is bound to appear. That, by the way, is a collective attitude."

The peace conference was a galvanizing experience for Milton, the kind of divine sign he'd been waiting for. Here was his destiny; he would be not just a socialist writer, but a writer of and for the proletariat, whose style and substance perfectly embodied the scientific teachings of Karl Marx. He re-evaluated his decision to become a poet, and set a goal that was both political and artistic: "to raise the entire human race to the spiritual level of poetry." Over the next year, Milton immersed himself in Montreal's socialist subculture, and eventually made his way to the Cooperative Commonwealth Federation. The CCF had been formed in Regina in July 1933 as a left-wing response to the Depression, and was made up of groups like the Socialist Party of Canada, the League for Social Reconstruction (a group of academics headed by Frank Scott), and the "Ginger Group," a collection of Progressive MPs, most of them farmers. While Milton was delighted with the chance to watch Frank Scott in action, it didn't take him long to figure out the CCF wasn't for him. Milton was a hard-line communist at heart, and Stalin himself openly assailed social democrats as no better than fascists. One year after the formation of the CCF, the Communist Party of Canada issued a response. Entitled *Soviet Canada is the Only Way Out for the Labouring People*, this manifesto declared that the CCF's promise of "socialism through parliament" was "only a device for maintaining capitalism." Obviously, there was a pronounced anti-communist sentiment in the CCF; Milton quit the party, as he later explained in a letter to Frank Scott, because he "certainly wasn't an anti-communist and didn't intend to be mistaken for one."

Milton moved on to more extreme pastures, and by 1956 was a card-carrying member of the Labour Progressive Party, the Canadian branch of the Communist International, which had been formed in 1937 when the Communist Party was still officially outlawed in this country. For Milton, this was a bold political statement; he was openly siding with an unpopular organization. The Rosenbergs had been executed three years earlier, scapegoats in the anti-communist fervor that swept the West; the Korean War had come and gone, and already communist forces were making inroads in Vietnam and Cuba. Milton's political stance was heroic, and a testament to the power of his imagination; although his lifestyle had changed little, he'd transformed his image from that of an introverted, middle-class kid to a working-class hero, a proletarian writer defending social truth in the face of fierce opposition. Milton's struggle for identity was a typical stage in the development of any artist, especially in Canada where physical labour is idealized and artists are often looked upon as unproductive members of society. But while his tough working-class image was in part a reaction to social perceptions, his commitment to Marxism and communism was heartfelt. In a touching letter to Mary, he reveals the genuine optimism that fueled his politics:

> In my room here I have two ornaments which are my own. There is *The Canadian Peace Calendar*, and there is the photograph of your kids. The two decorations are connected: one reminds me of people closely tied to me by the bonds of blood and affection for whom I hope and pray the world will turn out a better place than it has turned out for me; the other reminds me that my wish for them is only one with my wish for the world—and indeed, if peace and a decent life does not enter into the lot of the world's people within the next ten or twenty years then my wish for them is equally impossible. Supposing I was a

father (how often I read the papers and thank God I'm not! For more than one reason!) I might be looking at my children now and swearing that their lives would not be as unhappy as mine. How many fathers have sworn the same thing from the beginning of time? How many have their plans collapse before the machinations of the warlords and of the dealers in poverty and exploitation?

While communism appealed to Milton's political side, his artistic sense was drawn to the official party philosophy of dialectical materialism. "Dialectics is the science of the philosophy of contradiction," he once explained in an interview with *Intrinsic* magazine, as he unwittingly pointed a finger at dialectics' convoluted nature. It is a complicated philosophy which originally referred to a kind of logical conversation based on contradictory arguments. In the early 1800s, the German philosopher Hegel expanded dialectics to the level of a natural law; history, physics, and philosophy were all driven by dialectics, the swing from one point, thesis, to a contradictory point, antithesis, and finally, to synthesis, a union of the two. It's less important to understand the complexities of this philosophy than to realize that it was widely accepted as *the* underlying process of nature, a scientific constant as much as a method of critical analysis.

In the late 1800s, Marx and Engels turned to dialectics in search of a philosophical framework for materialism. In 1925, the Communist Party posthumously published Engels' incomplete *The Dialectics of Nature*, a book which explored the three laws of dialectical materialism which the writer had "abstracted" from the "history of nature and human society." The following year, the Third Communist International embraced these ideas as its semi-official philosophy, perhaps because it lent a scientific air to the irrational world of politics while justifying the new class system which arose within the movement, a system which granted special status to the military and bureaucratic elite. Being the good socialist, Milton Acorn embraced dialectical materialism. But while other young politicos struggled to understand the near-religious mysteries of the dialectic, Milton found it to be a key to understanding his own, ongoing emotional turmoil. His heart was full of love; his head was full of anger. These two contradictory forces waged an endless war inside him. Through dialectical materialism—a natural process, the ebb and flow of contradictions—eventually, something greater would be created, Milton could tell himself.

With dialectical materialism as its philosophical base, it's no wonder communism held such a powerful appeal for Milton; he could sum up his entire emotional experience and his thematic base as an artist in one simple contradictory phrase: in love and anger. But Marxism didn't just direct Milt's approach to writing poetry; the philosophy directed his approach to being a poet. "I had to establish the trade of poetry," he told *Intrinsic*. In other words, he had to take poetry out of the hands of academics and other bourgeois elitists, and create a framework where an ordinary man or woman could earn their living writing poems. That meant that the future held no cushy university jobs or nine-to-five grinds for Milt: if he was going to do it the right way, he'd have to do it the hard way—through his poems alone.

———

Milton continued to contribute to *New Frontiers* throughout the first half of the 1950s. While much of this work has been forgotten and very little was ever collected, it's clear that Milton was quickly maturing as a poet. The Fall 1953 issue had two Acorn poems in it: "Jack and the River," written in the conversational style of "Grey Girl's Gallop" although much shorter, and the sonnet "Norman Bethune, died Nov. 13, 1939." In this second piece we see a different kind of poet emerging, one more consciously literary and with a tone of complete self-assurance. Milton Acorn had found his voice:

We carried him who'd often carried us—
Spiritually, by purpose, and by scorn
Which rooted in his love, could just be borne. . . .

This poem is still rough, with Milton given to the old-fashioned habit of sacrificing line to rhyme, but it left an impact on the poet: thirty-one years later he re-worked it and included it in *The Island*

Means Minago. The Spring 1954 issue of *New Frontiers* included Milt's "To Cote's Statue of Louis Riel," and by now he was using his own name, identifying himself as a Montreal "carpenter and poet." Two issues later, the magazine published "He Lived on Life" and one poem by his friend Louise Harvey, "From Door to Door." *New Frontiers* wasn't just bringing Milt the valuable exposure and confidence a young poet needs; it was also broadening his scope as a reader and introducing him to the tradition of radical poetry in Canada. Radical poets often work outside of mainstream literary movements; Archibald Lampman, for example, died before the turn of the century, yet wrote in a kind of early-modern style, while Joe Wallace, the most important radical poet of the 1950s, wrote in the same working-class, oral tradition of people like Dawn Fraser. Joe Wallace was a regular contributor to *New Frontiers*, and in 1953 the magazine published his second book of poetry *All My Brothers*. "One of the most widely-read poets of our time is a writer of protest and prophecy," Margaret Fairley wrote of Wallace, adding that he had "many fore-runners. The names Blake, Burns, Shelley, William Morris, Bernard Shaw come first to mind."

Wallace was born in Halifax in 1890. Early on he worked in advertising, and was a member of the Young Men's Liberal Association until one night, when he was giving a speech, he was confronted by a left-wing heckler. Wallace was intrigued with what the man had to say, and soon after converted to communism. In the 1930s Wallace moved to Montreal, where he became an active member of the Communist Party, and even taught Marxism to Norman Bethune. After the war broke out, the government sent Wallace to Petawawa Internment Camp near Ottawa, where he got into trouble for arguing with a guard who questioned his patriotism: "I'm no Russian, I'm a Canadian," Wallace protested, earning himself twenty-eight days in solitary confinement. While there, he composed several poems, including his famous, stirring labour ballad "Your Arm is Strong Enough":

> Your arm is long enough
>   To reach the stars,
> Your arm is strong enough
>   To break all bars. . . .

By the late fifties, Wallace was one of Canada's best-selling poets although many of his sales were to communist readers: his 1958 book *The Golden Legend* sold 10,000 copies in both Russia and China. No Canadian poet since Robert Service—another writer in the oral tradition—had sold that many books, and none would come close again until 1971, with the publication of Milton's *More Poems for People*. There's no question that Milton was influenced by Wallace and his writing. In a 1975 interview for *Contemporary Verse II*, Wallace said that he'd been so impressed with "Grey Girl's Gallop" that he "wrote an enthusiastic review" for the *Montreal Tribune*. Milton told Wallace that when he read the review he "broke down and wept." Likewise, in a 1974 interview with *The Western Voice*, Milton credits Wallace as being the man who "convinced" him to become a poet, although he turned it into a backhanded compliment: "If this fellow is a famous poet," he remembered thinking at the time, "I certainly can be, because I can do better than that." (Although, in a later interview published in the Fall/Winter 1987 *Canadian Poetry*, Milton acknowledged Wallace's influence, and called him "a much underestimated poet" who had "published many admirable poems.")

History has proven Acorn to be the better writer; however, in the mid-fifties, the form and content of his writing bore the unmistakable stamp of Joe Wallace. In its four-year existence *New Frontiers* published ten of Milton's poems, including a short piece entitled "On Heros" under the name "P. Nutt." His final appearance was in the Summer 1955 issue which included a sonnet as well as a letter of support from Milton, pointing out how he particularly "enjoyed the various articles on the Indian background of our national story," and lamenting "I don't know what I'd do without *New Frontiers*." The poem was called "The Rosenbergs," and while it was Milton's most mature work to date, he wrote it in the classic sonnet style of fourteen lines with alternating rhymes, and a simple, direct voice that suggested the spell of Joe Wallace:

> Remember this, our comrades, if we die:
> It's not because we under-rate this world
> That we wont buy it with a stoolie's lie,

O not with hauteur, not with thin lips curled
Against assaults upon our purity,
Do we defy this awful threat we must;
But in our not-so-lonely hearts have we
A dam of truth that holds a sea of trust.

A dam which would have broken had we lied
So though we'd lived you wouldn't call it life
To dwell with memories of wasted strife
On frozen beaches, emptied by the tide,
Where coming greyly like a winter squall
Pale patient death would find us after all.

———

The year 1956 was one of turmoil and consolidation for Milton Acorn. Typically, it was a year shrouded in mystery, yet one which left him with a confidence in his writing that went beyond youthful bluster, and a stronger sense that his destiny was to be not just a working class poet, but *the* poetic voice of Canada's oppressed masses. The year started on a good note. For the first time in ages Milt had a steady job, in the CN Rail's express office. He told his friends that he was actually considering staying with this job for life. Soon after, Milt ran into an old friend, a woman he'd known on The Island. They had a brief affair, and within a year, the woman bore a son, who was soon put up for adoption. For a time, the two considered marriage, but then decided against it. For Milt's part, he was a man of old-fashioned values, who could barely provide for himself; how could he provide for a wife and child? More to the point, he was a man who had, by design or nature, set himself apart from the world, and whose demanding personality made it difficult for anyone to maintain a close relationship with him. Milt believed that adoption was the best option for his son, but it broke his heart to lose the boy. He also deeply regretted his inability to work things out with the boy's mother, a woman whom he considered his perfect opposite; "how dialectically mated we were," he wrote to describe the relationship, in "First Wife Sonnet."

In the midst of this turmoil, Milton continued to pursue his writing career. Bolstered by his success at *New Frontiers*, he boldly explored new territory within his writing, and new markets for his poems. Once again, as a young poet looking to get published, Milton couldn't have found a better place to be than in Montreal. It was the heyday of the so-called "little magazines" like *Contact*, *CV/n*, and *Delta*, which offered a more literary and "serious" outlet than Margaret Fairley's eclectic magazine. In a country where art is often shunned and ridiculed, these little magazines were the backbone of Canadian poetry, providing a forum for serious poets.

It's no accident that the rise of "little-ary" magazines coincided with modernism, for the new poets were committed to shattering the Canadian cultural elite, and they perceived the few established magazines which printed poetry as being enemy territory. But there was a practical reason for the rise of little magazines as well. The advent of inexpensive printing machines—first mimeographs, and later photocopiers—meant that anyone could put out their own publication. Like the introduction of inexpensive, high-quality recording equipment in the 1980s, which fueled the independent recording boom, these portable presses fueled the modernist movement: poets could now "do it themselves," and no longer needed the literary establishment to publish their poems. One of the first little magazines to catch Milton's eye was *Yes*, edited by John Lachs, Glen Siebrasse, and Michael Gnarowski under the guidance of Louis Dudek. In the first issue of *Yes*, Gnarowski outlined his magazine's philosophy, which offers today's reader a snapshot of the poetry movement at the time:

> A new magazine has come to Montreal. Perhaps the thought of a city that could clothe its people in the periodicals it sells does not make this seem an impressive accomplishment. Yet a distinction must be made here; for the professional efforts that roll their paper like two-legged beavers are quite apart from the phenomenon known as the "little magazines." These productions, such as Fredericton's "Fiddlehead," are not devoted to making money (heaven forbid), but rather to providing a stimulating and indispensable literature. Especially in such fields as poetry, which is

not commercially attractive, this need is fulfilled. Their other important contribution lies in the fact that they give encouragement to new talent by allowing them a medium in which to present themselves; people who, one day, might add weight to our cultural progress. Unfortunately the little magazine movement in Canada has shown a tendency to lapse in recent years. It is to be hoped that this mimeographed effort will initiate a new phase of activity in this field so as to provide a suitable outlet for the commencing Renaissance of Canadian Writing.

The new modernist movement wasn't just a rejection of outmoded poetic form; at its very heart it was an assault on the Canadian political and cultural establishment. The new poets believed that they were undermining power at a basic, cultural level. Michael Gnarowski is an English professor at Ottawa's Carleton University; in the early fifties, he was a student at McGill, and found himself immersed in modernism. "We were waging a war against the *Frygians*, the gang that was influenced by critic Northrop Frye," Gnarowski says. "We wanted our poetry to reflect the true nature of this country, and were tired of the social club poetry of Anglo-Saxon academic elite. We wanted poetry rooted in the ills and the pains of the society." This revolutionary tone was tempered with a home-made feel: in the first issue's editorial, the typist forgot the word "movement," and it had to be hand-written afterwards in every copy; meanwhile, "writers everywhere" were invited to submit their work to "Mike Gnarowski, 5050 Roslyn Avenue, Apt. 9, Montreal, P.Q." *Yes* captured Milt's interest. He regularly sent poems to Gnarowski, and in the fall of 1956 Gnarowski accepted one, although it wasn't published until the following year. "Lyric" represents a landmark in Acorn's development. Gone were the rhymes, politics, and narrative of his earlier work, replaced with the consciousness and the craft of a literary poet. And not surprisingly, love was on his mind:

> If I said love that word
> 'd recreate me as love;
> said love you that breathe

'd drop me trembly on
your breasts, your breath. . . .

Gnarowski and Acorn soon became friends. They'd meet once or twice a week at El Cortijo, in an area of town that was part working class, part student ghetto. In those days, Gnarowski worked in an office near the Stock Exchange, the very heart of the capitalist world. At night, he'd change out of his grey flannel suit and put on something more appropriate for the café, where he'd often hook up with Acorn. They were an odd pair. "Milton was extremely left wing, and I was something of a cold warrior," Gnarowski recalls. "So we had these great debates about communism versus western society. I used to taunt him about his so-called working class disposition and sympathies: 'Why the hell don't you get out there and work?'" While Gnarowski and Acorn were poles apart when it came to politics, they saw eye to eye on literary matters. The Romanticism of the past had outlived its purpose, and now it was time for a new kind of literary vision, one that spoke to and of the realities in the modern world.

Gnarowski remembers Milt nervously presenting him with a copy of his first book, *In Love and Anger*, late in 1956. Milt had inscribed it "To Mike: A damned reactionary, who also has an ability to enter into another man's creative process." Milt had paid for the printing himself—a normal practice for beginning poets, who often self-publish a number of "chapbooks" in the hopes of attracting some attention—and the book featured illustrations by Quebec artist Robert Roussil. While *In Love and Anger* was no bestseller, it did serve its purpose. Writers and, more importantly, reviewers took notice. Louis Dudek, perhaps the most influential critic in Montreal, offered a reserved but encouraging review in the August 1957 *Canadian Forum*. Dudek, who knew Milton and had hired the young poet to babysit on a few occasions, criticized his lack of discipline and a tendency to overwhelmed his poetry with politics. However, Dudek concluded that Milton would "make his mark" once he found a "personal frame for his anger and revolt."

There were sixteen poems in *In Love and Anger*, varying in length from the sixty lines of "The Dead" to "Remembering," which contained only a single couplet: "I saw a myriad glittering points of dew in

spiders mesh;/and I thought of the trail of your fingers on my flesh."
For the most part, the poems are awkward, the rhymes forced. They
seem to be a step back from "Lyric," and many were written before it.
Milton was struggling to be a good modernist—Thoroughly Modern
Miltie—and his subjects are certainly taken from the everyday world,
but he cannot make the break from traditional poetic structures. In "I
Must Go Back," for example, Milton sings the praise of the working
man, but in a way that would have pleased the ear of any turn-of-the-
century Romantic:

> I must go back to those good springs,
> The cleansing springs that flow from toil;
> To heal my hands in the soil,
> and know peace which labor brings. . . .

The poems reveal Milton's true nature. For all his talk of revolution,
he was a Romantic at heart, and had a wide conservative streak in him.
And while on the surface his political stance seemed extreme, I think it
was an expression of a Romantic longing to make the world a better
place, and was as much an idealization of the North American worker
as it was an expression of Marxist collectivism. In Milton's vision, the
workers unite, take control of the means of production, and find the
kind of satisfaction in hard work that had always eluded him. Mean-
while, Milton shows that the scars of Charlottetown had yet to heal. In
"I Will Not Love Too Much," he addresses the "Old Man"; it's a poem
undoubtedly directed at his father:

> I will not love you too much,
> Old Man,
> I will not love you too much;
> For yours is a mortgage type love,
> Old Man,
> that may be foreclosed any day. . . .

In fact, Milt's relationship with his father had began to improve.
While communism remained a point of departure, Robert Acorn was

mellowing with age. It became Milt's habit to return to Charlottetown
like a perverse Canada goose every winter, setting up shop at his par-
ents' home. In a curious way, he'd separated his family from the rest of
his social world. In Montreal, he rarely spoke of his family and almost
never discussed his childhood or even his beloved Island unless it was
in general political terms. When he wrote back home, he'd rarely
mention friends, and then only when they somehow related to his
work or politics. When he'd come home to The Island, he remained
the outsider, the relative stranger from some place else, and everyone
understood that he would be leaving again soon.

David Hooper was just a kid when Milt left Charlottetown; he
remembered his uncle as something of a mystery. "He was always
somebody who was away," David told me. "One Christmas, this great
big toy truck arrived from 'the Uncle in Montreal'; that was how he
was described to me. He was always spoken of with some adjective
attached to his name." When Uncle Milton came home to visit, he was
awarded special status; the normal family rules seemed not to apply.
David recalled him visiting in the mid-fifties. Milt was sitting at the
dinner table reading a newspaper when he suddenly shouted out:
"Damn capitalist Bastards!" These were the first words David ever
heard come from his uncle's lips. "Grandma admonished Milton,"
David says. "But he said, 'They're going to hear it anyway, they might
as well hear it now.'"

While *In Love and Anger* showed promise and a remarkable range,
only one poem stood out. Again, Milton's family provided the subject,
although the finished product was completely different from "Old
Man." The poem was called "To My Little Sister About Her Illness."
In tone, it was closer to "Lyric" than it was to the other works in the
collection, and it marked Milton's first attempt at the kind of visionary
poems that he would write over the course of his life:

> Know then, my little sister:
> that where black seas crash against riven rock
> their roaring drowns out neither life nor thought;
> that in the stronghold of endurance
> the coins of life are counted one by one;

and sometimes in the pauses of the storm,
when the sun strikes many-colored on the battlements
of new clouds rolling westward on their thunders
a glory can strike you
greater than a lightning bolt.

This poem transcends labels like modernism and Romanticism, springing from an older tradition of ecstatic poetry that came to Milton through Yeats and his careful readings of the Bible. It's a kind of poetry defined by its effect on readers (and listeners, since it's tied to the oral tradition); by the end, Milton evokes a certain mysterious joy, which points to an order and design beyond the human. "To My Little Sister About Her Illness" was a great leap forward for Milton, proving that not only could he write, but that he had the potential to take his artistry to the highest levels.

CHAPTER SIX

Moments

From the vantage point of our own tranquil era, the old history of the
human race reads like the annals of a race of maniacs. . . .
　　　　　　　—"The Last Lunatic," unpublished short story

ON AN INDIAN SUMMER DAY IN 1956, so the legend goes, Milton Acorn
had a revelation. In an instant, he decided to sell his carpentry tools and
devote his life to poetry. After thirty-three years wandering the wilder-
ness of self-doubt, Milt saw his destiny with clarity. He half-expected
some mighty sign from above, but the inspiration came from within: "I
came to"—as he would later write in "Pastoral"—"on numb, clumsy
wings,/to find outside the beauty inside me." The biblical parallels in
this episode are impossible to ignore. Was not Christ a humble carpen-
ter, thirty-three when he began his ministry? Was He not rejected in
His own land? Persecuted? Misunderstood? Did He not fight the
corrupt powers that had oppressed his people? There was something
messianic in Milt's self-concept, and he did daydream about becoming
a great revolutionary leader, but as much as anything, these allusions
were a product of his sense of irreverence that others often mistook for
conceit. The legend does leave out a little bit of relevant information. "I
couldn't get very much carpentry work because I didn't speak French

very well," he told the authors of *In Their Words*. "I could speak mainly for jokes, mostly a queer language I'd made up myself." Moreover, Milt never enjoyed the work, and often complained that the solitary life of the carpenter wreaked havoc on his delicate nerves.

But Milt did sell his tools. It was his first definitive step toward establishing the "trade of poetry in this country. It is a Canadian legend," he told *Intrinsic* magazine in 1979, "that this poet, Milton Acorn, sold his tools (he was a carpenter before) and swore that if poetry was not a profession he would make it one." He took his hammer and saws to a pawn shop on St. Antoine Street and made the sale as witnessed by his friend and fellow poet Al Purdy. The two had met a few months earlier when Milton appeared out of the blue at Purdy's apartment, softly explaining that an acquaintance, Irving Layton, had sent him. "He told me you wrote plays for CBC and could give me some tips," Milt said. Purdy invited the odd-looking man in. "I walked in the door and Purdy immediately wanted to talk about communism," Acorn recalled in *In Their Words*. Purdy concurs. "The subject of drama rarely came up," Purdy told me when I interviewed him at his home in Sidney, B.C. "We talked about poems, argued about poems, mostly." By morning, they were friends, already discussing the possibility of working together.

Purdy's house is a stone's throw from Georgia Strait, the ocean passage running between Vancouver Island and the mainland, and, incidentally, the ironic inspiration for the name of the alternative newspaper which Milt helped start. I found it hard to believe that Purdy was just a few years away from his eightieth birthday; he was lively and thoughtful, eager to open a couple of beers and talk. But I felt a little intimidated as well; Purdy has a slightly menacing air to him—the kind of man who, I was certain, does not suffer fools well. As I sat on his couch I thought how he and Acorn must have seemed like an odd pair in their day. Al was tall and lanky; Milt was shorter and broad. Al was extremely well-read, articulate, a social animal, something of a lady's man and a bit of a hell-raiser; Milt was well-versed in communist rhetoric, shy, and had a difficult time with women. Al was long married, and already eleven years a father; Milt was full of longing, and had already lost a son. Al drank beer; Milt favoured wine. And while Purdy was no neat-freak, he remembers going over to Milt's room on St. Antoine Street and being appalled: "There were papers and half-written poems, books and garbage piled up on the floor almost to waist-level; you could hardly get around." Despite their Mutt and Jeff appearance, the poets had much in common. Both were largely self-taught—literary renegades who would go on to forge careers outside of the academic world. Both lived in poverty and were between jobs as often as they were at them; like Acorn, Purdy suffered bouts of depression, sometimes lasting weeks, although his blue moods had more to do with near-poverty than any pathological condition. The contradictions of their relationship weren't lost on Purdy. In his 1994 autobiography *Reaching for the Beaufort Sea*, Purdy writes that he and Milt "were a strange pair to become good friends":

> . . . the friendship depending partly on mutual need and fellowship, but also because Milton was in the process of changing into an exceptionally fine poet. I rather sensed this about him, although there was little evidence to support the feeling on my part. He'd published *In Love and Anger* at his own expense, shortly before I knew him. It was, in simple terms, a bad book. The language was cliché-ridden, the sentiments expressed were often sloppy, and his grammar was almost as bad as mine. But I emphasize his continuing metamorphosis into—if not a butterfly (how could Milton be a butterfly?—it boggles one to think of it), into a sturdy, honest and emotionally moving poet. . . . The magic thing about Acorn was this change in him—the continual becoming, his chrysalis splitting. But his every day and every hour appearance remained exactly the same. The guy was a slob, and my own superiority in mentality, in manners and in personal hygiene was so obvious that I wouldn't acknowledge what was important to him at that time. . . .

Al Purdy was born in Wooler, Ontario, near Trenton, in 1918, of "degenerate" Loyalist stock. Like Milton, he began writing at age thirteen. At seventeen, in the height of the Depression, Purdy hopped a freight train headed west and made his way to Vancouver. By the time he met Milton, Purdy had already published three chapbooks and had written a dozen radio plays, although CBC producers had only accepted one. Milt would later say that Purdy convinced him to sell his tools and take up poetry fulltime, but Purdy doesn't remember talking Milt into anything. But he did influence Milt's decision. In a letter Milt wrote shortly after meeting Purdy, he talks of an opportunity that has come up out of the blue. "A fairly established writer invited me (it took a lot of urging, actually) to become his collaborator," Milt wrote. "He can guarantee my board, actually he has a lot of money from a bequest, and it looks like we'll be together for quite a while. Al is quite confident our collaboration will be a profitable one." Milt went on to write that the book would be called *The Crafte So Longe to Lerne*, after a line in Chaucer, and his own section would be titled, rather anachronistically, "The Unreconstructed Bolshevik." He was excited by the project, and was certain it offered financial success as long as his political enemies left him alone. "Even tho we put the struggle of man back into the first century BC someone is liable to see the implications of freedom on the present day," Milt wrote in his letter. "Those mystifiers know very well what they're doing. They know very well what they call freedom is no freedom at all, and even to talk specifically or analytically of politics arouses their suspicion." Bolstered by the confidence he gained in publishing his own book, invigorated by the anticipated patronage and friendship of an "established writer"—and encouraged that, at long last, his fight for a full army pension would soon be won—Milt decided to quit his job at the CPR and sell his tools. Purdy thought he was making a mistake. "Even a great writer like me can't make a living at it," Purdy told Acorn. Milt looked at his new friend for a moment, then replied: "Maybe *you* should buy the tools."

———

The collaboration didn't work out. Purdy proved to be too different a poet for Milt's tastes—the Ryerson Press would publish Purdy's *The Crafte So Longe to Lerne* in 1959—although their friendship remained intact. Instead of devoting his life to poetry, Milton was back hustling for odd jobs, fighting for his pension, and writing whenever time, and his neurotic temperament, permitted. He flirted with the idea of becoming a full-time science fiction writer, and while he got encouraging rejection letters from the likes of *Story Annual* and *Galaxy*, no one bought his stories.

"I have to break into fiction," he wrote to his mother, expressing his frustration. "The trouble is that my damned worrying neurosis gets in the way, and I don't produce as much as I should. That's the main reason I haven't succeeded yet." Milt's attempt to break into the sci-fi market seems blatantly commercial, but in fact it had a political undertone. In the fifties, science fiction was considered on the cutting edge of popular writing, and its readers were characterized as intelligent and subversive. For Milt, science fiction was a means to comment on current political and social injustices; it also allowed him to explore his own conditions in a more direct way than poetry allowed. A case in point is "The Last Lunatic." This unpublished short story is set in the year 2898 AD, in a world where death and misery have been eliminated—or have they? The colonization of Venus is in fact a government cover story to hide the systematic elimination of all undesirable elements of society: the old, the infirm, the mentally unbalanced, the politically subversive. The hero of the story is Craig Alayn, a lonely outsider, whose clarity of vision is defined as "insanity" by the powers that be. He's locked up in a sanitorium, waiting to be shipped "to Venus," as two doctors discuss his case. "You must not confuse his ailment with that old condition of feeble-mindedness—that is almost obsolete too," Dr. Omar says. "This man really has quite a high intelligence. He understands all right, as far as the words go. But it is quite likely that he reads twisted implications and distorted context into the text. The meanings he takes will always harmonize with his own particular delusion." Milt's tongue was firmly in cheek when he wrote this story, but the theme was one that fascinated him. What was the nature of "meaning"? Who determined "reality"? And what were the political imperatives of the people who made these judgments? One thing was certain: authority had its own agenda, and despite his flights of madness, the only vision Milt could trust was his own.

Despite Milton's forays into science fiction, something was happening to his poetry; it wasn't just improving, it was exploding. His landmark "I've Tasted My Blood" appeared in the April 1958 issue of *Delta*, and within a year more than twenty poems appeared in other "serious" literary magazines like *The Fiddlehead* and *The Canadian Forum*. Milton had found his success by completely inverting his formula. He'd tired of modern poetry, of what he termed, in a letter to Purdy, the "extreme subjectivism" and "chaotic dressed-up imagery." But he couldn't bring himself to completely reject modernism, and reached a compromise. Instead of writing about modern subjects in a Romantic manner, he took on the Romantic world of nature and love, and explored it in free verse. The titles tell the tale: "Inland Gull," "The Island," "Islanders." For inspiration, Milton had turned to The Island of his youth; it was an idealized place, where Milton's real-life role of outsider was transformed to that of observer, and where, among the birds and seas and trees, vestiges of working class glory could be found. To this neo-Romantic mix, Milton added a dash of dialectics. He cut away every ounce of flab from the philosophy, and was left with the simple idea of opposition, of images in conflict. The effect was stunning, as shown in the original version of "I Shout Love," a poem which, in a later, much-expanded version, would become Milton's most famous work:

> I shout love in a blizzard's
> scarf of curling cold,
> for my heart's a furred, sharp-toothed thing
> that rushes out whimpering
> when pain cries the sign writ on it. . . .

Milton was unfazed by his "sudden" success. He'd spent a decade trying to make a name for himself as a writer, but when it finally started to happen, he took it all uncharacteristically in stride. Perhaps it was his ego at work; he believed himself a great writer, and therefore it was only a matter of time before people took notice. But maybe he found his literary achievements a little hollow: his growing reputation was no different from his years of obscurity; rent still went unpaid, bills continued to accumulate, and he was as hungry as ever. Besides, he was still torn between poetry and science fiction, although the latter market was proving impossible to crack. As the rejection slips piled up, he grew frustrated with American magazines. He decided to fight them head on, and enlisted Purdy's help. Together they would publish a science fiction magazine that would use Canada, as he wrote to Purdy, as "an enclave from which to attack the American SF market with stuff bolder than any of the other mags." It would be fantasy with a social consciousness, and Milton suggested the title *Gulliver's Mag;* it would be a literary giant in the lilliputian science fiction world. Purdy was lukewarm on the idea, and as an aside, suggested that he'd like to start a poetry magazine along the lines of Michael Gnarowski's *Yes,* which was about to fold. Acorn liked the idea, and in that moment *Moment* was born.

Purdy and Acorn produced *Moment* in the living room of Al's Linton Street apartment, on a mimeograph machine Milt had liberated from the Labour Progressive Party. The format was primitive—sixteen legal-sized sheets, stapled together—but the content was impressive: along with the comments and reviews, the first issue featured poems by a future who's who of Canadian letters: Acorn, Purdy, Raymond Souster, Louis Dudek, Irving Layton, Malcolm Lowry, and Leonard Cohen. In the opening paragraph, the poets introduce their brainchild on an unsuspecting public:

> MOMENT'S A WAY OUT TYPE MAGAZINE WHICH PRINTS (PARDON . . . MIMEOGRAPHS) POETRY, OPINION OR FICTION . . . ESPECIALLY GOOD STUFF THAT NOBODY ELSE'LL USE. IF YOU HATE IT WRITE AND TELL US TO STOP CLUTTERING UP YOUR MAILBOX. IF YOU LIKE IT WRITE AND TELL US SO, MAYBE ENCLOSING A BUCK OR SO. THERE'S NO CHARGE AND (CURSE IT) NO PAYMENT.

The magazine had its desired effect. Purdy and Acorn finally found a regular forum—or more accurately, irregular, since *Moment,* like most little magazines, was published only when the editors found the

time. It also published a lot of younger poets like Joe Rosenblatt.
Rosenblatt would eventually win a Governor General's Award for his
poetry and become editor of *Jewish Dialog*, but in 1960, he was a
twenty-seven-year-old writer aching to see his work in print. "Milton
came along at a very important time in my life," Rosenblatt told me.
"*Moment* published my stuff, and Milton read my stuff. He was a good
critic. Fair. And he nourished people." After only a few editions, the
magazine was attracting attention. Acorn and Purdy sent it to poets,
critics and editors around the country—anyone who was on a mailing
list they could beg, borrow or steal—and soon people were wondering
just who the hell these literary renegades were. As if he anticipated this
interest, Purdy devoted some space to introducing himself and his
co-editor to their readers. With tongue in cheek, he described himself
as a "modest and self-effacing genius," then offers a critical, humour-
ous and deadly accurate portrait of his co-editor:

> Milton Acorn is concerned to get his point across (in most of his
> poems) with the minimum of verbiage and the maximum effect
> (who doesn't?); but the divergence between intention and result
> often culminates in flat failure. One accepts that any subject is
> material for poetry (I do anyhow), but the manner of subject
> presentation is the jam-it-down-their-throats school, it's good for
> you and that's all there is. He forgets a poem is a poem, and must
> be considered on its own successes or failures. There is seldom
> illustration of this thesis, but the thesis itself is raw and smoking
> and frequently unpalatable. In the pieces expressing social rage
> and political views there is a school-masterish talking down, in-
> flexible opinion, ponderous vehicular movement of ideas seem-
> ingly concerned to roll over and crush the unwary reader with
> slow page-turning reflexes. Any allusiveness on Acorn's part has
> such strongly implied meaning and intention that delicacy is an
> accidental byproduct; his metaphors are weapons that crush; his
> images, birds that are likely to shit copiously on the reader—the
> one with slow page-turning reflexes.
>   Maybe any defect has its characteristic virtues. But qualify that
> by adding that Acorn's defective methods sometimes produce

shining lights rather blinding in their intensity. . . . These things tie in unescapably with his social vision—large, sometimes bull-headed, with infrequent unequivocal nobility. And wherever this path of development leads the shambling, dull-eyed poet, it is not a blind alley.

With a couple issues of *Moment* under their belts, Purdy and Acorn left Montreal. Purdy quit his job at a Johnston's Mattress Factory on the spur of the moment, and moved to Ameliasburgh, in Ontario's Prince Edward County, near where he'd grown up. His wife Eurithe stayed behind to "keep the home fires burning," working as a secretary. Two years earlier, with money he'd earned selling three plays, Purdy had made a $300 down payment on property at Roblin Lake, a mile outside of town, and started to build a house. Now he returned to finish the house, and brought Milton with him. He was excited at the prospect of working with a real carpenter, since by his own admission, he could "barely saw a log." Together, they put in the A-frame cross-pieces, the skeleton of the house, with Milton leading the way. But Purdy noticed that the pieces were not level. "I had to take them all out after he left and put them back in again," Purdy recalled in our interview. "I'd never seen his handiwork before, but I had to conclude that if he was a carpenter, which he always said he was, he certainly wasn't a very good one."

When they weren't working on the house, they filled their time arguing. "For two months we quarreled over socialism, poetry, how to boil water," Purdy wrote in "House Guest." Milt concurred. "I couldn't even persuade him that a rafter had a top and a bottom," Milt said in *In Their Words*. "It took us two days to lay a line of rafters across one room. It was very irritating. It was a question of my patience and Purdy's impatience." Even in friendship, Milt sought out adversaries; something in his nature directed him always to the fight, and in Purdy he'd found a worthy, and tireless, opponent. This particular moment in time left a strong impression in the minds of both young poets; Acorn, like Purdy, felt the urge to set the record straight in the poem, "A Profound Moment in the History of Canadian Poetry":

Arguing the craft so long unlearned
At Roblin Lake, Ameliasburgh, me and my pal
Purdy fought; leaving no stone unthrown:
About internal rhyme, off-rhymes and thought-rhymes
Plus other quirks that work sometimes, hard-earned or
        suddenly known. . . .

Milt was only three years away from his fortieth birthday, but he could still feel self-conscious in unfamiliar settings. A case in point was the national poetry conference Queen's University sponsored in the summer of 1960. Milt heard about it while at Roblin Lake, but stalled when Purdy urged him to go. "I don't have any good clothes," Milt complained, for once unusually concerned about his appearance. Purdy replied: "That doesn't matter a damn. All poets are poor." Then he realized that Milt was simply afraid to go, feeling that he didn't belong in the company of Canada's esteemed poets. Finally, Purdy talked him into making the trip. He drove Milt to the main road and left him there to hitch a ride. Two days later, a rough-looking Milton showed up at Roblin Lake. When Purdy asked him how the conference went, Milt was evasive. "He finally admitted that he hadn't gone to the conference," Purdy recalled. "When he got to Kingston, he couldn't bring himself to go to any of the events. He just stood outside the lecture hall, hoping someone would recognize him. At night, he slept on a park bench. I guess he couldn't stand the thought of taking the chance to have all those great poets reject him." Here was Milton Acorn in a nutshell: both brash and shy, a human contradiction, longing to belong but not knowing how to join. He knew he had talent, but felt out of place among Canada's best-known poets.

After the disappointment at Kingston, Milt stayed a little longer at Roblin Lake, but eventually, as he always did, he outstayed his welcome. They had one argument too many—something to do with eggs, Purdy thinks—and that was it. Milt asked for a ride to the main road, where he could thumb down a drive. And so he was gone, and the house at Roblin Lake fell strangely silent.

CHAPTER SEVEN

The Embassy

> The exproletarian poet
> reclined on a deck-chair,
> sipped highballs provided by a millionaire
> and composed lines about despair.
> —"Epitaph," unpublished

MILTON PUBLISHED *MOMENT* #3 in the spring of 1960 from his parents' place on Prince Edward Island. Now that he and Purdy had parted ways, he was left alone to carry the torch: "For the moment," he wrote on the cover page of the magazine, "the editorship is one man." Milton had gone back to The Island to recharge his batteries, and to try and figure out his next move. During his decade in Montreal, he had lived in a dozen boarding houses and apartments, and crashed at friends' places a dozen more times when the money ran out. Politically, he was moving as well. Throughout the early fifties he had clung to the Labour Progressive Party—even as the Soviet communists proved themselves no better than any other imperialist power. Nineteen fifty-six was a watershed year for socialists: first, the new Soviet leader Nikita Khruschev denounced the abuses of Joseph Stalin, then Russian tanks rolled into Hungary to crush a socialist revolt. Milton quit the LPP in

1958, after careful consideration of what was "the most painful decision" of his life, citing Stalin's crimes and the authoritarian rule of the LPP leaders as the reasons for his decision. "The great majority of members of the LPP are very honest people," Milton wrote to his mother. "They have, like you and I, seen the absurdity and cruelty of the present capitalist system, and have been bold enough to envision a new system, in which the exploitation of many by man, which we imagined to be the root of all evil, would be abolished." After leaving the Communist Party, Milton flirted with various socialist organizations: the Socialist Party of Canada, the Socialist Forum, and the League for Socialist Action. Still, the move from the LPP weighed heavily; he had spent more than ten years of his life defending, almost deifying, the Communist Party. In secret, he wondered if this was the beginning of the end of his heroic struggle for political Truth.

Within a few months of publishing *Moment #3*, Milton had moved to Toronto to, as he later told *Intrinsic* magazine, "establish the trade of poetry." It was a good place to be, politically; the League for Socialist Action, among other groups, had its headquarters in Toronto, and the city that had long been the conservative stronghold of Canada was opening up to a wider range of political possibilities. Of course, the move was made easier by the full army pension he now received, which had been granted on the basis of his "bad nerves." It wasn't much, just a few hundred dollars a month, but it was enough to live on as he wrote his poems. In Toronto, he could supplement his pension by doing the odd reading for CBC radio or one of Raymond Souster's monthly Contact poetry evenings.

Souster was one of the few Toronto poets admired by the Montreal modernists. His verse was sparse, straightforward and eloquent, and dealt with images and themes from everyday life. While his lifestyle was fairly conservative—he worked for the Bank of Commerce for four decades—he was not part of the Upper Canadian academic elite and in fact was the only poet of reputation in those days operating completely outside the university world. Souster started his first little magazine, *Direction*, in 1943, after getting out of the Royal Canadian Air Force. Ten years later, he joined forces with Louis Dudek on *Contact*, a magazine dedicated to modernist poetry and modeled on the

seminal American literary magazine *Origin*. Although Souster and
Dudek only published *Contact* for two years, it was very influential
and led to the formation, with the help of Irving Layton, of Contact
Press, which was devoted to publishing new Canadian poets. The
weekly reading series was an offshoot of Contact Press; Souster wanted
to create a forum that would bring together people from all walks of
life who had in common a love of poetry.

Milton's first public reading was for the Contact series in 1960, and
took place at the Young Men's Hebrew Association in Toronto, at the
corner of Spadina and Bloor. Milton hadn't quite made up his mind
whether to leave Montreal, and this trip opened his eyes to the financial
possibilities for poets in Toronto. But his weren't the only eyes to be
opened. Outside of Montreal, Milton had a limited reputation, and few
knew what to expect from him. I can only speculate on what he read
that night—no records of the evening exist. Undoubtedly, he began
with a few proven crowd favourites like "Charlottetown Harbor,"
then just as the audience had made up its mind that he was a talented
but quaint "Maritime" poet, Milton might have delivered a sucker
punch. Around that time, he'd just completed a poem about his child-
hood passion, boxing. Called "The Fights," it displayed a power and
maturity that would have caught his audience completely off guard:

> What an elusive target
> the brain is! Set up
> like a coconut on a flexible stem
> it has 101 evasions. . . .

It was at one of these Contact poetry readings that Milton met John
Robert Colombo, a struggling poet and graduate student. The two
would often get together for coffee, and it might have been at one of
these sessions that Colombo mentioned the Bohemian Embassy, a new
club that was opening in town. "The Embassy," opened its doors on
June 1, 1960. It was the brainchild of Don Cullen, an enterprising actor
with a passion for the performing arts. The club was stuck on top of an
empty garage on St. Nicholas Street in the heart of Toronto's artistic

community. It served "poisonous coffee" (in Gwen MacEwen's words), hot cider (non-alcoholic), doughnuts, and date squares, and featured folk music, movies from the National Film Board, and on Thursday nights, poetry readings. There was a hint of rebellion to the Embassy; Cullen constantly battled the city, which wanted to close him down for operating without a license. He got around the need for an expensive restaurant permit by calling the Embassy a social club and charging patrons fifty cents for a year's "membership." Folk singer Sylvia Tyson was the resident musician; she would open and close many of the poetry evenings, and while she enjoyed her nights at the club, she came to see herself as the "comic relief." "Everything was deadly serious," Tyson recalls. "The place was full of lots of young hot shots from the University of Toronto." An evening at the Bohemian Embassy offered a mixed bag of entertainment, and the crowd was never exactly sure what would happen next.

One night, Miss Libby Jones, a "college-educated $1,000-a-week vaudeville stripper," dropped in to give a little taste of her performance and lecture on practical economics. "On the one hand she spoke of the 'defeatist dogma associated with Beatnik clubs,'" wrote reporter Anthony Ferry in the *Toronto Star*. "On the other hand, Miss Jones admitted that 'entertainment levels on this continent are pretty low.'" As soon as Miss Jones left the stage, Ferry reported, "a blunt, sun-beaten poet from Prince Edward Island" took over. "Acorn is a gifted nut who refuses to put his talent to the use of pretty images," Ferry wrote, "but prefers a violent image to make poetry out of shock tactics. His verse would rock Miss Jones, but it mostly tells a hard truth."

John Robert Colombo was "Literary Manager" of the Embassy. In fact, as Colombo recalls, Milt was the reason he took the five-dollar-a-week job; sure, he was interested in the literary scene, but what Colombo really wanted was to keep Milt at bay: "He didn't have a job, so he had a lot a free time on his hands. He would think nothing of dropping by our apartment early in the morning or late in the evening, wanting to chew his stogies and guzzle beer and discuss poetry. Not particularly the writing of it, but the reception of it. The writing of it was glorious and mute, but the reception of it was bloody and verbose.

He was always being rejected, and even when he hadn't submitted poems he knew he was going to be rejected."

Milton loved the limelight of the Bohemian Embassy, and soon became one of its resident poets, along with the jazz-inspired George Miller. His readings were well-attended, and he found in the college student crowd an appreciative audience. "On stage, he was unbeatable for the first fifteen minutes," Colombo says. "After that, he had to be excused. He glowed when he sat on the stool on the dais, under the light, surrounded by these tiny little tables, with anywhere from two to eighty patrons. He'd suck on the crook of his cigar and hold forth on whatever happened to irritate him, every once in a while reading a poem." Clearly thirty-seven-year-old Milton had found a place where he felt he belonged. He practically lived at the Embassy, and could be found there any hour of the day, writing poems, talking and teaching. He was the Senior Poet, offering editorial advice and old-fashioned encouragement to the circle of young poets who gathered around him—people like Margaret Atwood, David Donnell, Joe Rosenblatt, and a teenaged Gwendolyn MacEwen.

Milton also found the time to continue *Moment*. Issue #4 came out in September 1960, and demonstrated that Milton's critical capacities were growing along with his artistic ones. In an essay entitled "Open Letter to a Demi-Senior Poet," addressed to "Dear Dylan" Thomas, Milton created a Canadian framework for Olson's "Projective Verse." Milton's essay was widely read in its day, and would eventually find its way into Louis Dudek and Michael Gnarowski's classic 1967 book, *The Making of Modern Poetry in Canada*:

> I think the philosophical root of our disagreement lies in your assumption that there is an inviolate something called "poetry," that specimens of poetic art can be measured up against an essential standard and accepted or rejected on the grounds of whether or not they fit the definition of "poetry." I'm against that. Poetry is only a convenient label for a kind of creativity with words. A poem can be judged only on the basis of whether it is *something* or *nothing at all*, not on whether or not it is "poetry." To me, this is inseparable from the idea of freedom. I know a while back I was

telling everyone who'd listen that poetry was indubitably speech. I went farther and said that as far as I, the poet, was concerned, poetry was "direct speech." In time I found myself writing stuff which while still speech, was far from direct. What was I to do? Snip off a finger here? A brain-lobe there? (A DVA doctor once offered to arrange the brain-lobe job for me—I'd be so peaceful!) By snipping get myself back into proper definitional shape? I decided to ignore the definition for a while, and concentrate on the poetry—tho I always kept my mind on communication.

And in fact I've read fine poems by Eli Mandel, and one by Phyllis Gotlieb, which were hardly speech. And now I've come across good poetry—stuff that has a message—by Charles Olson, which is not speech by any possible definition. Yes, Olson, that's the itchy spot. To you he is an offender against your Sacred Goddess Poetry. To me he is an innovator in the science of poetics, the first to deeply analyze—in modern terms—the poetic line as spoken, not printed. Also, as noted above, he's made advances in another type of poetry; that which literally cannot be spoken. His work, in the spoken aspect, has been carried forward magnificently by the whole Beat movement, from Creeley to Corso. . . . These Beats have it. They're the true heirs of Sandburg and Fearing, the poets with large American souls. If their work is often ugly, blame it on the ugliness of present day America. . . . I see bad and good in them, but don't allow anything to blind me to the fact that they are an important movement, perhaps the most important movement to come on anywhere since the war. Equally, I don't allow their importance to blind me to the worth of Canadian poetry, which doesn't divide as neatly into "schools," which progresses more evenly, alert to the new—even helping create it as Layton and Dudek and Souster actually helped create the Beat school—but rarely losing sight of tradition. I think Canadians have much to learn from these Beats, and the younger American poets could learn much from us. Not that I'm hopeful they will; after all, Canada doesn't have a large enough army for the Yanks to pay too much attention to us.

Shortly after *Moment #4* came out, Acorn's second poetry collection, and his first "professional" book, appeared. *The Brain's the Target* was published by the prestigious Ryerson Press, and edited by Al Purdy (who'd suggested the book to Lorne Pierce, the rather staid United Church minister who ran Ryerson). Around the same time, John Robert Colombo's Hawkshead Press released *Against a League of Liars*, a single-page "broadsheet" containing fifteen poems cut from the original Ryerson manuscript. To help Milton earn some extra cash, Colombo gave him 100 copies, which the poet sold from the dais for twenty-five cents apiece or best offer. These two publications, particularly *The Brain's the Target*, established Milton as a poet of both talent and enormous potential. The fourteen poems included most of his best work to date: "Islanders," "The Island," "Charlottetown Harbor," "The Fights"—a line from which provided the book's title—and "At El Cortijo." Critics were struck with the diversity of subject and style in such a slim volume. Some took it as a lack of focus; others saw a poetic craftsman. Taken together, the book and the broadsheet enhanced Milton's stance as the Modern Romantic, whose tight, lyric poems celebrated nature, art, and love. Milton was also finding a voice for his political sensibility, but again, it was through compact poems, short story fragments really, offering glimpses of working class life far more effective than the Stalinist rhetoric that coloured his conversation. In the broadsheet's "Pit Accident," for example, Milton tells of the death of a young miner, using a restrained tone and attention to ordinary details to keep the poem from becoming overly sentimental:

> "I liked him," said the small man
> with coal seaming his hard little hands,
> "because he never stood in your light." . . .

Acorn's anger is subdued in these two collections, and at long last, he seems to have reached a truce with his father. In "The Trout Pond," Milton's "whitehaired" father becomes just another figure in the natural landscape, no longer a source of anxiety. When the anger does show through, it's tempered with an air of longing. In "Letter to My Red-headed Son," written to the son he'd given up for adoption in 1955, Acorn set himself apart from the world, a "poet, against a league of liars," while recognizing the limits of his vision:

> Fool poets call the spring green, but I
> a poet, know I can't give you to yourself
> —only what I know of myself: that
> nothing I've done, no poem, stand,
> thought or act of love, hasn't called for
> another, stronger deed, or I've lost it.

For a man used to keeping the most superficial details of his life a secret Milton proved to be remarkably honest in his poems, and showed much more self-awareness than many might have expected. It's as if, in the act of writing, he found the heroic courage he'd always searched for, the courage to look at himself honestly without flinching, and to try to discover the truths buried underneath the layers of myth. He was now approaching the height of poetic skills. His greatest triumphs, and most resounding losses, were just around the corner.

CHAPTER EIGHT

I Shout Love

I shout Love ... Love ... It's a net
scooping us weltering, fighting for joy
hearts beating out new tempos against each other. . . .
　　　—"I Shout Love," from *The Fiddlehead*,
　　　　　Spring 1963

EVERYTHING WAS FALLING INTO PLACE. Milton's work was finding criti-
cal acceptance, while he was finding his niche at the Bohemian Em-
bassy. Six years earlier, he'd sold his carpentry tools; now, for the first
time, he felt that he'd established himself as a professional poet, per-
haps the first true professional poet the country had ever seen. And he
was teaching a whole new generation to follow in his footsteps. He was
also falling in love, and this time, he assured his friends, it was the real
thing. The woman's name was Gwendolyn MacEwen, a promising
young poet almost twenty years his junior. She was beautiful, with
long dark brown hair and almond-shaped eyes, and an exotic air, like
an Egyptian princess. They might have met as early as 1959, when Milt
visited Toronto for his Contact poetry reading. Gwen definitely went
to these readings, and perhaps first saw her future husband reciting
poems from the podium. There is also a chance that she went to

Montreal to visit him; Michael Gnarowski recalls seeing her there. In any case, their romance began in earnest at the Bohemian Embassy.

Things probably started innocently enough. Milt was, if not a father figure, at least a big brother to many of the young writers who drifted into the coffeehouse. Did Gwen modestly ask him to take a look at some of her poems? Milt would have gladly obliged, giving the young poet some helpful and encouraging feedback. Over time, Milt certainly took an interest in Gwen's writing, and became her poetic mentor, and sometime later still he came to the realization that he wasn't just interested in her poetry; he had fallen in love. People talked about them behind their backs, calling them "Beauty and the Beast" and boldly predicting the relationship wouldn't last. Milt heard the talk, but discounted it as idle gossip.

Gwendolyn MacEwen was born in Toronto on September 1, 1941. She'd had a difficult childhood, according to *Shadow Maker*, Rosemary Sullivan's 1995 Governor General's Award-winning biography. Gwen's mother Elsie was a manic-depressive who spent much of her time in mental institutions and attempted suicide several times. Once, when Gwen was eleven and the family was living in Winnipeg, her mother slit her own throat with a straight razor, then went after her father. Gwen's father Alick was a frustrated photographer who once had a picture published in *Life*, and worked for Kodak as a film salesman. As the years of dealing with his wife's mental illness took their toll, Alick turned to alcohol for relief, and Gwen accompanied her father to Alcoholics Anonymous meetings. When she was twelve, her parents separated. In school, Gwen was an outsider; the kids called her "Space Lady," and she had few friends. When she was a little older, her father started showing up at her home, or at the Kresge's where she had a part-time job. By now, Alick's condition had completely deteriorated. He was a drifter who couldn't hold a job, an alcoholic who relied on his daughter for emotional support.

Young Gwen MacEwen took refuge in the worlds of magic, myth, and imagination. In her early teens she set her sights on being a writer, and just after her seventeenth birthday she saw her first work appear in *The Canadian Forum*. By eighteen, she'd already written her first novel. She must have been overwhelmed when Milton Acorn began to pay attention to her work. He was by then an established poet with a

powerful presence and a reputation for being unconventional, to say
the least; the perfect mentor for an ambitious young writer with a taste
for the unusual. "When Milt met Gwen," Joe Rosenblatt recalls, "he
was clean-shaven, he was calm, he was funny, he had an optimistic
outlook; there was none of the nuttiness." By December 1960, Milt had
already asked Gwen to marry him. She declined, saying that, although
she loved him, she was too young; the world and its possibilities were
just opening up to her. But Milt persisted, gallantly reminding himself
that a faint heart never won a fair maid, and in July of 1961 he con-
vinced her to join him on a holiday in the Laurentian Mountains. The
love affair blossomed, and Milt once again implored Gwen to be his
bride.

That winter, Milt left Toronto to spend Christmas on The Island.
While he was visiting at his sister Mary's house, the phone rang. It was
Gwen. "Yes," she said. "Yes, I'll marry you." When Milton put down
the phone, he let out a great whoop and danced across the kitchen
floor. Mary had never seen her brother so happy. But amid the out-
ward congratulations and celebrations, some people, including mem-
bers of Milt's own family, had concerns about the marriage. His sister
Kay sent him a letter from her home in Regina expressing her delight
over "the most wonderful news" she'd heard in years. "I always felt
sorry," Kay wrote, "that you never found someone to love you truly
when you have so much affection in your heart." At the same time,
though, she remembers talking to her boss. "I said 'I think her parents
are crazy for letting her marry him,'" Kay recalls. "You just couldn't
live with him. I mean, I loved Milt so much, but I just couldn't cope
with him. I couldn't cope with his pain. My boss said, 'Well, she's a
poet. She's probably as erratic as he is.'"

In fact, some of Gwen's friends did try to talk her out of the mar-
riage, but this increased her resolve, and on February 8, 1962, Milt and
Gwen exchanged vows at Toronto's City Hall. At first, Milt had con-
sidered an Anglican service, but he'd asked the minister to skip the
story of the marriage in Cana of Galilee, in which Jesus turned water
into wine. These miracle stories were nothing more than fairy tales,
Milt said, that defied all scientific laws. The minister refused to rewrite

the marriage service, so Milton Acorn took his business elsewhere. Gwen didn't mind, though; when it came to religion, she was drawn more toward eastern mysticism than western orthodoxy. The service was simple, with only Al Purdy and Gwen's mother there as witnesses. Gwen proudly declared: "Here we are Mr. & Mrs. Acorn, just a couple of nuts." The newlyweds immediately began work on *Moment #6*, and finished it within weeks. Both were listed as editors, with Gwen adding "Acorn" in brackets at the end of her own name; the mailing address was given as Apartment 4, 20 Dupont Street, Toronto.

In later life Gwen would deny having had anything to do with *Moment*, but her stamp is everywhere in #6. The magazine *looked* neater, for starters, and the number of typographical errors dropped off considerably. The editors added a graphic of three phases of the moon—undoubtedly Gwen's idea. She also contributed two poems ("Marine Affair" and "Pyramid Poems"), a review of Phyllis Gotlieb's *Who Knows One?* and was credited with an essay entitled "An Open Letter to *Tish*." Here is a clue as to why the honeymooners rushed the new *Moment* into print. Perhaps it was an effort to address some pointed criticism of *Against a League of Liars* from *Tish*, an upstart literary "newsletter" based in Vancouver. In a review in *Tish*'s December 1961 issue, entitled "Why Doesn't Someone Tell the Truth?" poet and critic George Bowering had taken Milton to task for his broadsheet. "It has long been held here that Acorn is the most promising of the newest generation of Montreal poets and nightclub readers," Bowering wrote. "But this collection is a disappointment. These are very young & very amateur poems. In fact, in view of their formal chaos, they are not poems at all, but rather editorial gripes set into 3-inch lines."

The review was fair comment; *Against a League of Liars* by no means represented Acorn's best work, although it's curious that Bowering chose to examine the broadsheet rather than Milton's more successful *The Brain's the Target*. I wonder if the controversy-conscious *Tish* group was taking a deliberate potshot at this "most promising" poet in hopes of generating a public response? Acorn was known as a hothead; how could he resist responding to such an inflammatory review? But it was Milt's old friend Al Purdy who entered the fray

first, firing off a response that was published in the next *Tish*. Bower-
ing's claim that "some statements will fit better into sociological disser-
tation than into free verse" particularly offended Purdy. He saw it as "a
stricture on what can be said in poetry and what cannot be said." But to
fully appreciate Purdy's comments, we have to back up.

Bowering was born in 1935, and was raised in British Columbia's
Okanagan Valley, a lush farming and fruit district along Okanagan
Lake in the south-central part of the province. After finishing school,
he enlisted in the Royal Canadian Air Force, where he worked as an
aerial photographer, and where he became friends with a budding
young poet, Richard "Red" Lane. Upon leaving the air force, Bower-
ing enrolled in the University of British Columbia, where he earned a
degree in history and discovered the possibilities of poetry. In 1961,
Bowering started working on his Master's degree in English, first with
the poet Robert Creeley as his thesis advisor, then under guidance of
Warren Tallman, another displaced American. That's when he joined
a group of fellow students and poets to start *Tish*, a group which
included Frank Davey—who was awarded the title Managing Editor
because he owned the typewriter—Fred Wah, and George Bowering.
Although the *Tish* group were seen as *avant garde*, they had a lot in
common with the new modernists and cited Raymond Souster and
Louis Dudek as inspirations. Like the Montreal group a decade earlier,
these Vancouver writers wanted to explore new possibilities in poetics.
The difference was that while the Montreal modernists were satisfied
freeing the language and structure of poetry, the *Tish* group was com-
mitted to exploring poetic structures and to openly debating the nature
of poetry. Where the Montreal and *Tish* poets differed most decidedly
was in their approach to politics. The older group, in its struggle for
"social realism," had a clear political stance which resulted in a com-
mon rhetorical position that ran through their poetry. The *Tish* group
saw poems as events in themselves, occurring despite any political
message they might carry. "Poetry should be listened to as a vocal event
rather than print, rather than rhetoric, especially rather than rhetoric
that characterized the poetry of the Montreal group," Bowering wrote
in a July 22, 1972 letter to the literary magazine *Blackfish*.

Because of their outspoken opinions, *Tish* found itself under attack from both academics, who saw them as intellectual pretenders, and poets. "The poets in the east were saying, 'What the hell's theory got to do with poetry?'" Bowering told me in a phone interview from his Vancouver home. "They believed that you're just supposed to open your hearts and thighs and write poems, and they were affronted by the fact that we were talking about poetry a lot, rather than laying it out like good Canadians. It was a kind of aw-shucks Canadian thing. That Canadians were considered natural loggers coming out of the woods, slapping down their feelings about bears and stuff. It was those pretentious Europeans who liked to *think* about poetry."

Tish marked a new era. The magazine represented the first conscious avant garde expression of postmodernism in Canadian poetry. This "postmodern movement," as it came to be called, was largely an American invention, with roots in the writing of Pound and, particularly, William Carlos Williams, and its philosophical base in Olson's "Projective Verse." (Olson perhaps even coined the term, in a letter to Robert Creeley dated October 20, 1951.) In the U.S., the postmodern era began in the mid-forties. As with previous poetry movements, postmodernism started as a reaction to the contemporary literary climate. In its day, the free verse political-and-social realism that characterized modern poetry had been revolutionary, but by the end of World War II it was accepted and entrenched. Enter the postmodernists—Olson, Duncan, Lawrence Ferlinghetti, composer-poet John Cage—who set out to once again invigorate poetry through experiment and a self-conscious, largely apolitical opposition to mainstream culture. "In general," writes poet Paul Hoover, in his introduction to the Norton anthology *Postmodern American Poetry*, "postmodern poetry opposes the centrist values of unity, significance, linearity, expressiveness, and a heightened, even heroic, portrayal of the bourgeois self and its concerns." To Hoover's mind, postmodern aesthetics like performance and language poetry are "simply the most recent of many attempts, including those of Wordsworth and William Carlos Williams, to renew poetry through the vernacular."

With its emphasis on language and sound, and its air of revolution, I would think that *Tish* would have appealed to Acorn. But Milt was not alone in his criticism of postmodernism. It's a cliché to say that in art and fashion, Canadians always lag behind Brits and Americans, and *Tish* flowered a generation-and-a-half after the seeds of postmodernism were planted in the United States. But to Canada's defence, modernism had a harder time taking root in this country than it had elsewhere, and was not truly established until well into the 1950s. Meanwhile, an impressive array of talented poets stepped forward—Layton, Dudek, Scott, Birney, Purdy, P.K. Page, Dorothy Livesay, Ralph Gustafson, James Reaney—to announce that we had a national poetry as strong as that of any other country. For the first time, there was a Canadian Voice; this voice, rather than any particular literary movement, became the standard by which Canadian poets were judged.

Poets like Acorn and a lot of others didn't like the way *Tish* emulated American writers. While Acorn could point to Olson as a source of inspiration, *Tish* more consciously imitated him and worked to put his theories into practice. "*Tish* is a moving and vocal mag," ran the editorial in *Tish*'s inaugural issue, immediately invoking the spirit of Olson. "Its poets are always obsessed with the possibilities of sound, and anxious to explore it meaningfully in relation to their position in the world." *Tish* regularly sponsored visits by so-called "Black Mountain Poets"—people like Robert Creeley and Robert Duncan, who were associated with Olson's Black Mountain College. In fact, a series of three lectures by Duncan provided the direct inspiration for *Tish*—Duncan even came up with the magazine's name, a phonetic inversion of "shit." Meanwhile, the group's mentor was a transplanted American critic and professor, Warren Tallman. To a nationalist like Acorn, *Tish* was far too American; understandably, *Tish* strove to be cosmopolitan. "Poetry is not an international competition," ran the lead editorial in *Tish 8*. "Let's have no more superficial jingoism in poetry."

In this light, George Bowering's December 1961 review of *Against a League of Liars* makes more sense. When Bowering complains that Acorn is "sadly tone deaf," he speaks from the perspective of a postmodernist, whose concern goes beyond the use of imagery based on everyday speech. "Poetry, as a specialized form, combines the statement of the poet & a commitment to sound as the vehicle of the statement," Bowering wrote, echoing Olson. "The latter is as indispensable as the painter's commitment to color. Acorn, it would appear, is committed to shock & simile, & is content to let sounds fall in a pattern characteristic of neither his language nor of poetry." Acorn responded to Bowering's review indirectly in *Moment #6*. I say indirectly because the "Open Letter to *Tish*" never actually mentioned the review, and the essay itself, although clearly influenced by Acorn and likely written by him, is credited to Gwen. In any case, it amounts to one most effective critique of that group of poets—*Tish*-ites included—who'd taken Olson's "Projective Verse" as gospel, and marks a departure in Acorn's own attempt to find a Canadian context for Olson's poetic theories:

> It sounds good, all right: natural rhythm, word clusters, breath and syntax control—but the proof is in the poet's pudding. And I get the impression from this end that you're using Instant Mix. Damnably, it's all too facile in this idiom for poetasters to grab only the essentials of the Olson-Jones school and produce almost convincing carbons. There are 2 limbs—take your pick: 1. Poetry that falls off a log and lends itself happily later to the breath-line premise, or 2. Poetry employing exclusively that premise and never getting an inch from the ground because such marginal concerns as craft and self-enclosure are thrown down the toilet along with your 'alien iamb'.
>
> Note One: After hearing a reading by and exchanging a few words with Olson—I got the impression he wrote his much-exaggerated "Projective Verse" off the top of his head. It's basically serious, but a standing joke. "Everyone," he said, "does something every day. One day I sat down and wrote that thing." Let's not wallow in that kind of irony too long. The great man himself knows this is not the whole pudding. Read "Maximus" and see what happens when you springboard up and away by using more of what centuries of accumulated music and language have given you. Granted, speech rhythms provide that fine vital undertone in poetry. And granted, Olson employs in readings the breath-line to its fullest advantage. But the printed page has no vocal

chords. You've got to do more than talk blithely about how you walked into a room and had an incredible urge to touch an object & etc. As well as being adolescent artiness, this is invalid poetry. *The poet begins with the reality of that object; being a poet, his relationship with that object is understood; he doesn't end there.* And let's forget about writing poems about a poet writing poems about a poet. *Art consists of concealing the craft of the artist, not elaborating tediously upon it.* Do you believe that just because you write Poetry you are Interesting and Important enough to write solely describing your own Divine Function?

———

Not long after *Moment #6* came out, Milt and Gwen moved to a rented cottage at 10 2nd Street on Ward's Island, a short ferry ride from Toronto's harbourfront. There were the odd skirmishes—plates were thrown—but there were also moments of great joy. At night by the fireplace, reading poems to each other until the wee hours of the morning; afternoons, dancing naked in the rain. She was his blushing bride, and he was, in her childish pet name, her "ephalent." David McFadden recalls that Milt had placed a scary-looking log in front of the house to "scare off the bill collectors." Inside the little house, tucked away in a corner, there was an old oak table set with a large candelabra. Above the table was a painting of an albatross crucified.

Milt loved life in the cottage. For once, he had a sense of permanence, a sense that after years of struggle, the simple pleasures that came so easily to everyone else were now his. You couldn't call the couple financially secure: Milt made $2,160 a year from his disability pension, while his mother meticulously managed his finances for him from her home in Charlottetown. Still, he and Gwen got by on the little they had. It was 1962, and Milt was at the top of his game. His skill as a poet seemed to improve every time he sat down at the typewriter, and—thanks to his regular stint at the Bohemian Embassy which had turned him into a minor celebrity—his self-esteem had never been stronger. He was moving beyond the little magazine and chapbook—six of his poems appeared in Eli Mandel and Jean-

Guy Pilon's prestigious *Poetry 62* anthology, and Irving Layton se-
lected "At El Cortjo" and "I Will Arise and Go Now" for *Love Where
the Nights are Long*, a collection of Canadian love poems. While he
was getting recognition within poetry circles, he longed to bring his
poetry and politics to a wider audience, and in July of 1962 he found,
literally, his soapbox. Things started innocently enough. One Sun-
day, Milton ambled down to Allan Gardens, a park at the intersec-
tion of Sherbourne and Carlton in Toronto. With a small group of
young poets in tow, he made his way to the statue of Scottish poet
Robert Burns. Milton took a journal from under his arm and began
to read:

> I shout Love in a land of muttering slack damnation
> as I would in a blizzard's blow,
> staggering stung by snowfire in the numbing tongues of cold,
> for my heart's a furry sharp-toothed thing
> that charges out whimpering
> even when the pain cries the signs written on it. . . .

The poem was "I Shout Love," although this new version was radi-
cally different from the original he'd written two years earlier. Since
then, Milton had overhauled the poem completely, eventually expand-
ing it to almost 170 lines, in a conscious effort to recreate the effect and
impact of Allen Ginsberg's "Howl" (and in the process, slipping effort-
lessly, and I believe unconsciously, into a postmodern aesthetic). Like
Ginsberg, Acorn was attempting to summarize the experience of his
generation in a voice that was immediate, original and personal. "I
thought I wouldn't write a *poem*," Ginsberg wrote in his liner notes to
a 1959 Fantasy recording of *Howl, and Other Poems*, "but just write
what I wanted to, without fear, let my imagination go." Here, Mil-
ton found a poet who shared his ecstatic vision, whose best poems
could transcend social or political messages and lead readers to spiri-
tual and emotional epiphany. In "I Shout Love" Milton piled layer
upon layer of imagery, abandoning literal meaning to a kind of
hypnotic truth. The result was stunning; a "postmodern" poem in
the Canadian voice:

I shout Love even tho it might deafen you
and never say that Love's a mild thing
for it's hard, a violation
of all laws for the shrinking of a people.
I *shout* Love, counting on the hope
that you'll sing and not shatter in Love's vibration. . . .

A few people stopped to listen to the poet as he read in the park. He had an air about him; a sense of authority. Although he wasn't tall, he was broad through the chest, and the rolled-up sleeves of his plaid work shirt revealed thick forearms which, if not shaped by a life of hard labour, seemed at least made for it. He wasn't handsome either, but neither was he ugly nor even plain; his wild hair was combed in only relative terms, his face at thirty-eight already lined and ruddy, but there was a dignity to his look and the small crowd responded to him. Within a few minutes, however, a plainclothes policeman came forward and asked him, politely enough, to stop his recital, and told the onlookers to disband. In that instant the Allan Gardens Free Speech Battle had begun.

Milton knew what he was getting into when he stepped onto his soap box and started to recite. He knew a city bylaw prohibited anyone from public speaking in a park without a permit, although in some parks, including Allan Gardens, religious sermons were allowed. In other words, you could preach but you couldn't teach; you could read a psalm, but not a song. Days after getting a ticket for his public reading, Milton organized a meeting at Don Cullen's apartment and most of the the Embassy crowd was there. It was undemocratic and patently unfair, Milton said, that some people could speak in the park while others were silenced. This wasn't just an issue for poets; everyone in this country had the right to free assembly and freedom of speech, and the City of Toronto was quashing their civil liberties. The issue was tailor-made for Milton and his cluster of young, idealistic followers; at stake was everything and nothing. By the end of the meeting, the group had made a decision: calling themselves "Interpoet," and embracing the principles of civil disobedience, they pledged to fight city hall to the end. Gwen had been with him at the first park reading and added her voice to the organizing meeting at the Embassy. She would miss the next few rallies, though, for she was leaving on a trip to Israel. Milt understood. She was young and needed to spread her wings, and the Middle East had always fascinated her. Let her go and enjoy her trip; it was only for two months. They would have the rest of their lives together.

CHAPTER NINE

Parting

How often in this bed
have I cried
'Gwen! Oh Gwen!'
Now I cry it
and the bed empty
except for me.
       —"Gone," from
          The Fiddlehead, Spring 1963

THE FOLLOWING SUNDAY MILTON SHOWED UP at Allan Gardens with a few more poets. The press was there too, and more than the usual number of cops that you might find in a public park on a lazy summer afternoon. Milton took his place by the statue, opened his Gideon's Bible, and turning to "The Song of Songs" he read:

Behold, thou art fair, my love; behold thou art fair; thou hast
     doves' eyes.
Behold, thou art fair, my beloved, yea, pleasant; also our bed
     is green
The beams of our house are cedar, and our rafters fir. . . .

Some people chuckled and clapped, others simply nodded and smiled. Milton was up to no good. A moment later, the Reverend Acorn put down his Bible and picked up his notebook. He launched into "I Shout Love," and raged on over the protests of the attending policemen:

> I shout Love to you, flesh humming thoughts, blood's rhythm,
> intricate bonework, hair played in by wind,
> and your words jostling, seeking
> things growing or still, peopled, mysteries, yourself
> with your soles touching the grass for instants. . . .

The cops weren't sure what to do. They ordered the poet to shut up, but still he raved on. They told the crowd to disperse, but the people didn't budge, and with every passing second, someone else joined the throng. The police feared that if they pushed too hard, things could get ugly. They decided to let Milton have his say, and then deal with him later. By the time Milton reached the end of his poem, he could taste victory. His voice became stronger, sterner; his time in the Anglican Young People's Theatre group was paying off. He turned to the police and addressed them directly, punctuating each line with a stern wag of his finger:

> Listen you money-plated bastards
> puffing to blow back the rolling Earth with your propaganda
>   bellows and the oh-so-reasoned negations of Creation:
> When I shout Love I mean your destruction.

After the reading, the poets lined up to give their names to the police and collect their tickets. And the following Sunday, more poets read more poems, and more policemen gave more tickets. By then, the Allan Gardens Free Speech fight was well-known around Toronto, and while many of the good city's good citizens looked down their noses at the collection of beatniks behind the fight, they saw the poets' point. Soon, a thousand people were turning out to watch the weekly "free speech party," and the man in the middle of it all found himself the centre of national attention. *Maclean's* wrote about the battle, and Milton was even invited to appear on the CBC television program *Front Page Challenge*, although he declined (to the relief of his sister Kay, who was afraid that he would be goaded into an embarrassing argument by the cantankerous columnist Gordon Sinclair).

Along with Milton, Joe Rosenblatt was a prime mover behind Interpoet. Rosenblatt was a regular at the Bohemian Embassy, and saw Milton almost daily. "He was the most self-tormented man I ever met," Rosenblatt recalls. "But at the time of the Allan Gardens he was at his sanest, and I think it the most exciting period of his life." Rosenblatt helped set up a benefit reading at the Embassy to help pay Milton's mounting fines—twenty-five dollars each, a hefty sum in those days, especially for an unemployed poet. "Milt got about a thousand summonses. I worked for the railway, and of course I couldn't afford to get too many summonses because I'd have to take time off work and I'd get fired. They had detectives there. At one point there was almost a riot there, and I had to appeal to the crowd to please settle down. They were going to attack the cops."

With battles raging on one front, Acorn resumed his war with *Tish*. Just before Gwen left for Israel, the two of them published *Moment #7*, "a magazine of poetry and . . ." The issued lacked the energy of earlier *Moments*—one review and one poem by Gwen, "Skull and Drums," no poems by Milton—and it's no surprise, particularly in light of what was to come, that this would be the final issue. It was centred around seven poems of a young Montreal poet, K.V. Hertz, and in the essay introducing these poems, Acorn ruminates on the nature of modern poetry while taking a swipe at *Tish*. "The Montreal Miracle and K.V. Hertz" was considered an important piece of criticism; Gnarowski and Dudek would include it too in *The Making of Modern Poetry in Canada*:

> Because, among other things, of the small size of the Canadian Army, Canadian poetry gets little recognition on the international scene. When Creeley was in Toronto he spoke publicly of Irving Layton, and in terms of the highest praise. Little reflection of this shows in critical works south of the border. The Beat

movement, with all its monumental faults as well as its virtues, has inundated all but the academics—to whom nobody listens.

North of the border, in Vancouver, we have the *Tish*-ites who—at this stage of the game—have taken the Beat philosophy, with its emphasis on creative freedom and imagination, and transformed it into the most rigid and sterile dogma you could imagine. They too remain deaf to Canadian poetry, including what has been done in their own local, and to mention the Montreal Miracle would no doubt send them into saliva-spraying fits of doctrinaire rage. Yet the miracle continues, and whether time will recognize it or bury it remains a side issue. It *is*. In an English small town buried in a French city, with an undigested mixture of national origins and truncated class structure, a vital independent poetic tradition has originated and revivified itself in each generation. A.J.M. Smith and Frank Scott kicked off the ball forty years and more ago. Purdy and Acorn got their essential training there.

It isn't ending today. . . . The tradition has maintained its identity. The Academic reaction of the forties and early fifties never had an impact in Montreal—or if it did the nibble was so slight it has been forgotten. The much more vital Beat movement has had little effect. Two characteristics distinguish Montreal poetry from all that has come and gone: (1) it doesn't think that the square world can be abolished by ignoring it; it remains in the midst socially conscious, socially critical; unlike *Tish* it doesn't reduce poetry to a contraceptive plaything: (2) *The poets learn their trade*. . . . One thing is certain. Despite all the dogmatic *Tish* talk about "commitment to voice" (what an abysmal degradation of that good old word "commitment") their examples fade, like a sordid dew, before the work of a poet who is genuinely committed. To voice, and to far more than voice.

Beneath the bitterness, Milton had genuine concerns. To his mind, the Romantics had ruined poetry by over-intellectualizing it and by establishing rigid rules of form, and now the *Tish* poets were making the same mistakes. Moreover, they had much disregard for the Canadian poets that came before them. Politically, *Tish* was all wrong as well. Here was Milton Acorn, struggling, with some success, to establish poetry as a legitimate profession; meanwhile a handful of bourgeois academics in Vancouver were telling him what a poet should and should not do. But what Milton failed to recognize was that *Tish* itself was caught up in a time-honoured Canadian literary tradition: giant slaying. Each successive generation of Canadian poets, it seems, has tried to establish an identity by dismissing its predecessors. The McGill Movement attacked the Romantics; the social realists of the forties attacked the McGill group for not going far enough; the new modernists of the fifties attacked the social realists for the same reasons—while all along, everyone attacked the faceless, nameless academic elite (despite the fact that most of them made their living at universities). That the *Tish* poets would take on its forerunner was nothing new: that they were unashamedly academic, apolitical and international—that's what really stung Acorn and his contemporaries.

Of course, the *Tish* crew was not about to let Acorn's latest assault go unanswered. In their very next issue, dated July 14, 1962, Frank Davey goes on the warpath, damning Milton for his ignorance and his central Canadian bias. But for all their talk against "superficial jingoism," there was a definite strain of regionalism to *Tish*. Here was a movement from Vancouver, aligning itself with a powerful American literary force, taking on a representative of the new Canadian poetry establishment:

> This month, again on these editors' front page, we get another dim-witted remark, this time to the effect that the "Beat" movement in the U.S. has "inundated all but the academies." As anyone with any sort of awareness outside of Upper and Lower Canada would know, the only true "Beats" were Kerouac, Ginsberg and Orlovsky. One could enlarge the definition to include all the contributors to *Beatitude* magazine, but even here we are getting into the region of hangers-on, or "beatniks." However, calling these people "Beats" is a minor sin in comparison to calling all the other non-academic poets in the U.S. as such. The idea of calling Olson, Ashbery, Koch, Lamantia, Creeley, Eigner,

Oppenheimer, Dorn, Duncan, Weiner etc. "Beats." How igno-
rant can an eastern Canadian be? Calling anyone writing in the
tradition of Whitman, Pound, W.C. Williams, Aldington, H.D.,
or Wallace Stevens "Beat." I ask, is William Carlos Williams a
"Beat"? H.D.? Robert Duncan? Denise Levertov? By this per-
son's definition ("creative freedom and imagination") I suppose
they are. Why I bet this nutty editor would even Beat his wife.
Such statements as his are pure literary irresponsibility—an
insult to any readers his magazine might have. . . . People tell
me that this man is anything but a scholar. In this case he
should not pretend to be one. As it is he appears to be a real
nut, a complete literary ignoramus—he even cannot spell
Creeley's name correctly. Perhaps someday he will take a taxi
ride out of Toronto. . . .

―――――

Gwen had left for Israel on July 10, four days before *Tish 11* came
out. In her absence, Milt decided that while the cat was away the
"ephalent" would play. Before the wedding, they'd agreed on an un-
usual arrangement, an open marriage in which either was free to take
another lover when the mood struck. Gwen was faithful during her
trip, despite men constantly harassing and propositioning her; she told
Milton of a fellow who tried to buy her favour with a lemon, but did
not mention how she was nearly raped by a twelve-year-old Arab boy.
But Milt had a fling in his wife's absence. He couldn't help himself; Joe
Rosenblatt remembers how women were always phoning him up and
asking him out. On her return to Canada in August, Milt confessed his
indiscretion to Gwen. It was nothing, he assured her, sensing, though,
that something was up. Within a month Gwen became involved with
an artist who lived on Ward's Island. Milt—according to the story his
mother told his sister Kay—demanded that Gwen choose between the
two men. The next day, Gwen moved out of the newlywed cottage.
Milt was bewildered, and blamed his marital problems on simple sex-
ual intrigue. Gwen was just getting back at him for his affair, he told
himself; she'll come crawling back soon enough.

What he failed to see was that Gwen had grown up on her trip. Rosemary Sullivan, Gwen's biographer, believes that the marriage was in trouble from the start, and from Gwen's perspective, effectively over before she left for Israel: "It must have been very hard on her, thinking that she was with a very solid man who was going to take care of her—I don't mean in the conventional sense. Here was this poet who seemed so strong, so confident. But it turned out that underneath the surface, Milt was a fragile figure that Gwen had to handle with kid gloves. The responsibility to take control of the family fell to her, and she didn't want it." There are whispers that Gwen left Milton because he was abusive or over-possessive, but Sullivan doesn't give these stories credit: "I don't think the relationship was physically abusive at all. You have to be very careful how you frame information, because suddenly it will be Gwen the victim being bullied by Milton. I got the sense that she was quite independent. And if they had verbal battles, I would imagine Gwen was just as tough as Milton."

Today, it seems like a relationship doomed from the start. Both of them were outsiders, and not the easiest people to get along with. John Robert Colombo remembers being astonished when this mismatched pair got married: "She was exactly the opposite of Milton: organized, neat; an angel from some Celtic heaven, descended on Anglo-Saxon Toronto and adding a grace note to it. But she was very ambitious at the time, and maybe she saw Milton as 'established.' He certainly suggested self-assurance, and Gwen could use all the self-assurance that she could get back then. In a funny way, I think she was also attracted to his instability." The difference in their personalities was clearly reflected in their poetry, and it's hard to imagine two more dissimilar writers. Milton poems were Romantic, his images simple, his best work driven by rhetoric; Gwen's poems were deeply intellectual, precise, and complex. In reading their poems, it's striking how little they seemed to have influenced each other.

In the years since their breakup, the brief marriage of Milton and Gwen has become the stuff of legends, often perpetuated by people who only knew Milton in later years after his mental and physical health had declined. In those sad days, Milt was "The Beast" to MacEwen's "Beauty"; how could she ever have agreed to marry him?

But these labels are unfair. Milt may not have been the most handsome man on Earth, but he wasn't ugly, and in the early sixties he had a charm, charisma, and popularity. However, his own self-image remained low; according to Rosemary Sullivan, Milt liked to characterize himself as a lumbering elephant, and his sister Kay said that even before the marriage he himself was using the "Beauty and the Beast" analogy. It was, after all, the perfect image for him: a dialectic fairy tale where the union of two contradictory people produced a love that transcended them both.

For Milton's part, it's easy to understand what he saw in Gwen. She was young and insecure, which instantly gave him the upper hand in the relationship. She was also pretty, which didn't hurt, and fed Milt's lopsided vision of himself as a heroic poet-knight, battling the dragons of injustice, and leaving the fair maidens swooning. Milt also craved the love, stability, and family life that marriage offered, and while his heroic fantasy might have been able to sustain itself through a brief romance, he couldn't hope to keep it up in a long-term relationship. But was there even more going on? Milt had come to anticipate disappointment, and while he ached for happiness, it was completely foreign to his experience, completely outside of his conception of himself. Here was a man who had fallen in love with a teenager, and who hoped to find some kind of permanence with a person who'd yet to establish her own identity. Was he setting himself up for defeat? Amid the greatest artistic and personal triumphs of his life, was he driven toward his greatest failure? One thing is for certain. At some point, if only for a moment, Milt and Gwen were a man and a woman in love. Milt had everything. Then, in the slow wink of an elephant's eye, he had nothing.

———

Milt did not take the breakup very well. At first, he wanted to believe that it was just a passing fancy, that Gwen would spread her wings for a while, then flutter home to him, begging for a reconciliation. But Gwen was firm in her resolve, and reality sunk in. John Robert Colombo remembers getting a phone call late one night: Milton was at the subway station, and he'd just broken up with Gwen. "Can I come over?" Milt asked. Colombo's heart sank. Milt was already drunk and depressed; he could do anything in that condition. "I finally said he could come over," Colombo says. "He just got drunker until he was incoherent. He didn't talk about the break-up once he got here. He wanted commiseration, sympathy, and solidarity. But he was devastated. It was like being granted three wishes, and then finding out that your third wish nullified the other two. Milt ended up in worse shape than when he started because he was bereft of the ideal he had. It wasn't a matter of love eluding him; he'd actually had it briefly and lost it, he felt, forever."

Milt left Colombo's house in the wee hours of the morning and wandered off into the darkness. He spent the next few days drinking and sinking further into his personal abyss. When Joe Rosenblatt ran into him, Milt seemed almost delirious, and talked openly of killing himself. Milt had written a poem on the wall of the Village Bookstore, a popular hangout for Toronto writers, expressing his inner torment; the poem haunted Joe Rosenblatt, and he's never forgotten it:

> I'm a silence so grim
> no sparrow can flutter in
> with its small music
> nor can a child's innocent rhyme
> touch me
> where a wish grinds on bone.

At one point, while walking with Rosenblatt along Davenport Road, Milt wandered off into traffic, and Joe had to drag him back to safety. He told Milt to check into Sunnybrook, Toronto's mental health hospital, but Milt refused. Two days later, Milt took an overdose of sleeping pills and wine. He was back in hospital again. All of Milton's old demons had arisen. Booze. Depression. Rage. Paranoia. Suicide. He became completely absorbed in his anger toward Gwen—one letter from that time begins with "You Dirty Bitch" and ends up asking "WHERE IN THE WORLD DID YOU LEARN TO BE SUCH A LOUSE?" Doctors kept him at Sunnybrook for several weeks, where he made at least one more attempt on his life before transferring him to Ward S2, the psychiatric wing of the Westminster Veterans' Hospital in London, Ontario. He spent the next seven months there, give or take the odd "escape," trying to piece his life back together. All in all, Milton found his stay useful, and was grateful for the help the medical staff gave him. In a letter to the Hospital Superintendent that he wrote in October 1963, Milton praised "the quality of the treatment" he received, and compared his stay favourably to his stint at Montreal's Ste. Anne De Bellevue Hospital ten years earlier:

> ...I couldn't help but be struck by the tremendous advances made in the treatment of the mentally ill. For example, in my last commitment the psychiatrist in the place thought it was his business to inquire into my personal beliefs and adjust my thinking to conform to the structure of society. As I was convinced that the adjustment of my thinking was not the problem, rather it was that the adjustment of society to meet the needs of human beings, this led to a situation where I had to soft-pedal my personal beliefs and pretend they weren't very important. Thus my relations with the psychiatrist were not honest. In the case of my stay with you there was no attempt to interfere with my beliefs. Indeed, I found a more democratic setup in which the patients had some say in the administration of the hospital. In this context I was, in the process of my recovery, able to assume something like the role I filled outside, and fight for the rights of my fellow citizens (in this case the patients). I found that the staff understood my role and did not resent my activities, rather they welcomed them. I found the hospital a much saner environment than any I had met outside.

Piece by piece, Milton began to build his life again. He got a major emotional lift from his father, who wrote him in hopes of settling once and for all their past differences. "I say without any reservations whatsoever that you yourself have nothing to reproach yourself for," Robert Acorn wrote. "You were a child and I was supposed to be the mature person, which I wasn't. I had a mental fixation of 'discipline' and 'mode of behaviour' which was impossible of realization. I love you and know you will eventually achieve peace of mind, and also go to great heights in the literary world." Milton found comfort in learning that, after years of struggle, his father had found peace of mind, and gently chided him for "nourishing useless guilt about" past troubles.

Meanwhile, as Milton recovered in Ward S2, his career was gathering momentum. Thanks to his efforts Toronto city council voted in favour of free speech in the parks. In the spring of 1963, in the wake of the publicity the protest generated, two new Acorn collections were released: a special Milton Acorn edition of *The Fiddlehead*, the prestigious literary journal put out by the University of New Brunswick's English Department, containing fifty-eight of Milton's poems; and, *Jawbreakers*, published by Raymond Souster's Contact Press. Although the collections overlapped—fifteen of *The Fiddlehead* poems also appeared in *Jawbreakers*—they introduced the main body of Milton's writing to a widespread readership, and signaled loud and clear to the Canadian literary community: Milton Acorn had arrived.

Jawbreakers had been in the works for well over a year before it was released. To hear Milt tell the story, the book's publication was a minor political triumph. In a 1986 interview for the *Cross Canada Writers' Quarterly*, he said: "Souster came down one day and said 'Milt, why don't you bring out a book with our press?' I said, 'OK, I'll get one together. It's time I got out a regular book anyway.' So I put out a book of forty or fifty poems called *Jawbreakers* and the Canada Council didn't want to print it. So Souster said, 'OK, if they want to be sons-of-bitches we'll print it ourselves.'"

The story behind *The Fiddlehead* tribute is more straightforward. In his introduction to the issue, poetry editor Fred Cogswell said that it all started with a letter from Joe Rosenblatt "to the effect that Milton Acorn's 'I Shout Love' was a great poem. After reading this poem, I was determined to devote an entire issue of *The Fiddlehead* to Milton Acorn's work." The timing of the two collections could not have been better. Milt had gained national notoriety for his role in the Allan Gardens fight, and while the reading public was intrigued by the poet with the curious name, many were put off by his politics and stood in waiting to dismiss Milton as an artless crackpot. A review by V.A.

Coleman in the June 29, 1963 edition of the *Montreal News Observer* reflects the public's mood. Coleman explained that "before the infamous 'Poet in The Park' fiasco, Milton Acorn had published one book and a broadside of poems," then concludes that Milton had progressed as an artist. "His hard protest poems no longer seem shout poems," Coleman wrote. "These are poems of and for the people en masse, social poetry, and he seems to have stepped down from his combination dynamite-soap box to bring them to us." Purdy picked up on the same note. He wrote to congratulate Acorn for *Jawbreakers* and added that the book would "do more good than all your navel admiring readings in Allan Gardens, for it's real and solid."

The critical response to *Jawbreakers* was overwhelming. Milton Wilson, an influential critic, counted it as the year's best poetry book, and there were rumblings of a Governor General's Award. Fred Cogswell, reviewing the book in *The Fiddlehead*'s Acorn issue, praised Acorn's "affirmative voice" and proclaimed that if Canadians were "not ready to listen and to be challenged by his humanity and his vision, they deserve the mediocrity which such dullness and insensitivity must inevitably bring." Meanwhile, *The Canadian Forum*, the most thoughtful and influential magazine in the country, included a long review of the *The Fiddlehead* poems in their March issue. Poet Bryan McCarthy praised Acorn's particular brand of "romanticism that never gives way to vagueness" and the simple humanity of his poetry. "The poems stand reading and re-reading," McCarthy concluded. "*The Fiddlehead* must be congratulated for devoting an issue to a poet who has not, as yet, been acclaimed as he deserves." Even George Bowering got into the act in a July 1963 review in *The Canadian Forum*, complimenting Acorn's "confident, deliberate, even-paced, and active" voice.

Milton's voice hadn't softened though, and he wasn't about to forgive and forget. He fired off a letter to the *Forum*, writing that it was "peculiar how a man with a divided mind betrays himself." He was particularly enraged by Bowering's suggestion that Acorn "collect a group" of his short lyric poems for publication. "As for the suggestion that I should bring out a book consisting entirely of castrated verse," Milton wrote, "no Mr. Bowering, I'll not join you or your claque of Establishment fairies. I'm perfectly confident that I can beat you." In any case, what impressed reviewers and readers alike was the range of Milton's style and subject. He first demonstrated his versatility with *Against a League of Liars* and *The Brain's the Target*, and the new collections were even broader. There were nature poems, short lyrical snapshots of The Island, love poems, ruminations on art, history and social issues; but most of all there were these visionary poems like "I've Tasted My Blood," the long version of "I Shout Love," and the remarkable "Sky's Poem for Christmas":

> As from milky vapor, dust of atoms jostling like hornets,
> a nebula swings great swatches of itself into a new sun
> raw with light, ravener to its parent mists, messenger
> to far astronomers thirsty for the word, the word
> that'll unlock them: I've never lost a faith
> or wrenched my roots of eyes from the heart. . . .
> Each doom to joy and torments nourished
> within an old love, becomes a new focus
> pulsing radiation, disrupting
> the foggy smut of death about it. . . .

By now, Milton was fed up with Toronto. "Homewreckerdom," he called it, and blamed his failed marriage on the city's gossips and back-stabbers, who he believed had talked Gwen into leaving him. He'd outgrown the city; Allan Gardens left him a minor celebrity, and despite himself, Milt was now a full-fledged member of the literary establishment. For a lifelong outsider, Toronto was getting awfully familiar. Milt had drawn a line down the middle of the country, he told friends. Gwen could have anything east of Winnipeg; everything west was his. So in November 1963, he talked Colombo into giving him a ride to the train station, and caught a train for Vancouver.

CHAPTER TEN

Into the Lion's Den

The truth is that I've hated
And the truth is that I hate continually
Day after day I bathe my brain
in suds of imagined vengeance.
—"After Eluard," from
The Canadian Forum, November 1966

MILTON HAD ESCAPED FROM GWEN, and from his own growing literary reputation, but in the process he'd marched straight into the lion's den. Vancouver was *Tish* country. Moving there, he felt, would allow him to attack Bowering, Davey, Wah, and the entire *Tish* gang head on. "In spite of my repugnance," Milton later wrote of the *Tish* group in a letter published in the Summer 1972 issue of *Blackfish*, "I was curious, and journeyed all the way to Vancouver on the conviction that where there was shit there must be animals." *Tish*'s status—and the city's—had been enhanced by the now-legendary Vancouver Poetry Conference held in the summer of 1963, which brought the full spectrum of American postmodern poets together for the first time. The presence of Ginsberg, Creeley, Olson, Duncan, and a host of others signaled that Vancouver was *the* place for poets. Milton did not arrive in Vancouver until four months after the poetry conference, and while he left very little record of his early days in Vancouver, we do know that he "found a fascinating group of downtown poets whom the *Tish*-ites were trying to put down," poets who lived and worked in the downtown core, outside of the university and *Tish*'s sphere of influence.

One of the first "downtown" poets Milt met was bill bissett, a young writer from Halifax who'd hitchhiked across the country in an effort to "escape Western civilization." When I interviewed him in his downtown Toronto apartment, bissett recalled running into Milt at Vanguard Books, a left-wing bookstore on Hastings Street. Although he'd only been in town for a matter of weeks, Milt was already organizing poetry readings in the Trotskyist hall behind the bookstore (where, rumour had it, he built the bookshelves). "Those were the first readings I ever did," bissett recalled. "Milt and I had a lot in common, politically speaking, and I was also open to accept some of Milton's behaviours that other people might have had a hard time with. I knew his kindness, and how he was helping young poets at that time." One month before Milton appeared on the scene, bissett had started his own political and literary magazine called *Blew Ointment*—named after a Victorian cure for venereal crabs. He produced the magazine in a little corner of his basement on a run-down Gestetner. By the time the second issue came out in December, Milton was a contributor, offering a short, lacklustre essay on newspapers ("One thing I like about the newspapers is it's possible to run with the hare and the hounds") which he'd given bissett to lend credibility to the struggling new magazine. Milton might have been a literary exile, but his name still carried a lot of weight.

By the time the new year rolled around, Milton was also close friends with Richard "Red" Lane, a maverick young poet and one of the more intriguing literary figures of the era. Red was born in 1936 in Nelson, 500 kilometres east of Vancouver, and spent much of his short adult life wandering B.C.'s interior and coast. Although his literary output was small—there were only a handful of books, most of them published after his death—almost every writer to emerge from Vancouver in that era seems to have a connection to Red. He read at the

Vancouver Poetry Conference, and was friends with George Bowering (they'd been in the air force together in the late fifties) although he was not part of the *Tish* crowd. Bowering remembers Red as a striking man, with plenty of charisma: "Everybody loved Red; he was just one of those people that everyone gravitated toward. He was a very protean kind of figure. He was strange-looking. He had orange-coloured hair and absolutely white-colored skin, and he was always on the edge of crime—sometimes over the edge. A lot of his friends were small-time, small-town hoodlums who went to jail from time to time." They became fast friends. Soon after their meeting, Milt visited the Lane family in Vernon, where he met Red's younger brother Patrick, another aspiring poet.

In December of 1964, Red Lane suffered a cerebral hemorrhage and died. The loss took the wind out of Milt's sails: he had another serious bout of depression. Red's brother Patrick, who'd just moved to Vancouver, became Milt's lifeline. The older poet became a fixture at the Lane household and an endless source of wonder to Lane's children, who called him "Uncle Miltie" and marveled at the way he made his dinner by slicing a loaf of bread lengthways, lathering it with an entire jar of peanut butter, and gobbling down. Lane came to dread the late-night phone calls, with Milt threatening to kill himself. Lane would take off in the middle of the night, searching the streets in the seedier parts of town for any sign of Acorn. During this time, Milt was harbouring the fantasy that he and Gwen could reconcile. On August 20, 1965, he sent her a letter from his Granville Street apartment, and apologized for not having written sooner. "I've been deeply troubled," Milt wrote, then added cryptically, "I hope it's not too late." What he didn't realize was that Gwen was working officially to annul their marriage.

In the fall of that year, Gwen wrote Milt, tiptoeing around the issue of divorce. "This is only a querulous letter about how you feel on the matter," Gwen wrote. "I had a good year money-wise, and I have some savings of a few hundred dollars. I'm willing to use this (if the idea suits you) in paying for any expenses involved." But the idea did not suit Milt at all. He scrawled "The Last Love Letter" across the top of Gwen's note, and banged off a reply, claiming that she would have no case if she took him to court that he had no intention of filing for a divorce. "I am no Don Quixote," Milt wrote. "I fight for love, I fight for freedom." But he *was* Quixote, the idealistic heroic lover, tilting at windmills. Beneath the posturing, though, Milt was hiding from the real issue. Gwen was clearly telling him the marriage was over. It was a truth he didn't want to hear. His stubborn refusal to grant a divorce kept the marriage technically "alive," and forced Gwen into the intrigue she so wanted to avoid. In February 1966, she snuck out to Vancouver to try and get evidence that would prove Milt had committed adultery (these being the days before no-fault divorce). Gwen spent her time in Vancouver avoiding Milt, and talking to mutual friends who told her that Milt had been seeing a teenaged girl named Myra. A few days later, she took her evidence back to Ontario, which she used, along with a deposition from Al Purdy, to finally get her divorce. A downward spiral of depression and booze started all over again and within weeks Milt was back in the hospital.

———

While Milton fought the demons inside his troubled mind, he found a new devil to battle in the outside world: the United States. Milton had always been a nationalist, but during his Vancouver years he transformed into a Canadian chauvinist with a hatred for capitalist America. The seeds of discontent were planted in the fifties, when he was trying to establish himself as a science fiction writer; after all, *Gulliver's Mag* was intended as an "enclave from which to attack the American" sci-fi market, while *New Frontiers* openly attacked "degenerate" U.S. commercialism. There was a strong sense of independence as the country pushed away from the economic and cultural domination of the fading British Empire. This was the era of the Flag Debates, and when the country adopted the Maple Leaf as its new national symbol in February of 1965, many Canadians believed that the nation had finally come into its own. Although Milton came from Loyalist stock, his hatred of the British Empire ran as deep as his disdain for Yankee imperialism. A letter Milton wrote to his mother shows the depth of his passion. "If you want to consider yourself an English pig go ahead,"

Milt wrote. "There is no English in me. I am not a thief. I am not a murderer. I have lived by my own efforts all my life and treated every human being as my equal as long as they behaved as equal.... You have been hitting harder and harder on this and getting more and more abusive on this question. That's the last. There is no relationship between you and me. You are no longer my mother." Fortunately, the relationship survived this battle (and many others that followed), but Milton obviously had some strong feelings about Britain, and particularly detested its position as a colonial power, which he equated to murder and oppression. He knew he had English ancestors, but nevertheless argued the point to the bitter end. It's a poet's logic: Britain was a colonial power, therefore immoral; Milton was virtuous, and therefore could not be British.

Milton was quick to pick up on the spirit of Canadian independence, and also sensed a growing threat from a new imperial power, the United States. American foreign policy had been largely isolationist until World War II, but since then the country had taken a more active role in the world. By the mid-sixties, the Bay of Pigs and the Cuban Missile Crisis had come and gone, and the Vietnam War was underway. The Canadian west coast became a haven for American draft dodgers, who joined with Vancouver's thriving socialist community to protest the American military involvement in southeast Asia. "The Vietnam War kept us hoping," says bill bissett, who was swept up in the social activism of the time. "We were constantly organizing rallies and readings, trying to raise money to support the North Vietnamese." But to people like Acorn and bissett, the most distressing thing about the U.S. was not the impact it was having on a tiny country half-way around the world; the Devil of Yankee Imperialism was encroaching upon their own backyard. *Tish* was just one example of how Americans were infiltrating the highest levels of Vancouver's intellectual and educational community. British Columbia had always been more open to American influences than the rest of Canada; perhaps the Rocky Mountains encourage North-South communication lines, or maybe it's just because Mother England was so far away. In any case, Milton could see the American influence everywhere he turned in Vancouver, and according to bissett, this made him uncomfortable. "Everything at all cultural levels was run by Americans at that time," bissett says. "And what wasn't run directly by Americans, was influenced by the strong 'pro-American' camp."

Meanwhile, in the midst of this anti-Americanism, a "new left" consciousness was evolving. Milton, whose "old left" communism had grown unpopular during the Cold War, found his politics relevant once again. Gabor Maté remembers Milt from those days. Today, Maté is a family physician, psychotherapist, and writer, but in 1966, he was a student radical whose activities brought him in contact with the legendary poet. He told me in a phone interview from his Vancouver home that Milton and his old guard politics were respected by members of the new left, although there were fundamental differences between the two groups:

> The Old Left was a working class movement, even though there were a lot of middle-class people in it. It was a working-class revolution in the Marxist sense. The New Left didn't come out of any working-class movement. It came out of a combination of the civil rights movement, anti-Vietnam protests, and campus reform politics, so it was essentially a middle-class student phenomenon. As such, it didn't have that sort of class outlook that the Old Left had. Nor was it a homogeneous unit; because it didn't have a predominant world view at its core, like communism, the New Left splintered pretty quickly. You have to remember too that there was no desperate economic situation for any of us. There was an abundant source of money in those days for students and youth—student loans and bursaries were growing on trees—and there was no question of any of us working when it was all over. So we could afford to play a lot more than people who grew up in that old left. That was a very serious bloody business; unions, scabs, and getting your head smashed in. And that's where Milton grew up.

It was the summer of 1966, and the hippie movement was in full swing in Vancouver. Maté recalls that students across the country had organized a national March of Concern, to protest rigid admission requirements at Canadian universities. According to Maté, University of British Columbia's students' council, "being very much of the Liberal-Conservative bent," had opted out of the march. But a group of students that included Maté, Karen Sorenson and her husband Peter Cameron, Gordon Larkin, and Randy Enomoto formed an *ad hoc* committee and forced a referendum on the issue. The students overruled their own council and voted in favour of UBC joining in the national march. Inspired by their political success, the core of this committee decided to find a permanent base.

They found an empty warehouse on 10th Avenue a couple doors up from Alma Street—in the UBC student ghetto on the cusp of Kitsilano, now a trendy neighbourhood, but back then, the heart of Vancouver's counterculture. They kept the name of the previous tenant—and much of the decor—added some tables, chairs and coffee machines, and in the fall, opened for business as the Advance Mattress coffeehouse. Milt immediately became a regular, hosting the Thursday night open-mike "Blab sessions" and frequent poetry readings with himself as the feature attraction.

In some ways, Milt was trying to recreate his glory days at the Bohemian Embassy (was it really only six years earlier?), but this coffeehouse was as a whole less interested in poetry than politics. But his weekly Blab sessions were the talk of the town, and Milt often used his turn at the mike to carry on his own anti-LSD campaign. He recognized the dangers of this psychedelic and the "morbid Learyite drug cult" that promoted it; he once took the drug himself, although not voluntarily. He was at a party, and someone spiked the punch with LSD. "It was a really remarkable experience," Milton told the *Cross Canada Writers' Quarterly* in a 1986 interview. "Everybody around me started turning into monsters. Not monsters in a vicious sense—into petit-bourgeois monsters. And I was going around denouncing everybody in some language that I fancied to be French." Meanwhile, his readings at places like the Advance Mattress, the Trots Hall behind Vanguard Books, and even at UBC and Simon Fraser University helped establish an alternative to *Tish*. In later years, he'd maintain that the breakup with Gwen had overwhelmed his creative capacities, and his artistic output during the Vancouver years was minimal, but Milton was actually at the height of his development as an artist. It's true that he didn't publish any new books during this period—a collaboration with bill bissett, *I Want to Tell You Love*, was completed, although publishers were turned off by the disparate styles of the two poets—but he was remarkably productive. Magazines like *The Fiddlehead*, *The Canadian Forum*, *Evidence* and *Blew Ointment* were regularly publishing his poems, as were dozens of now-forgotten little mags that sprang up throughout North America in the early sixties. Acorn's poetic vision had become darker, with titles like "Death Lyric" and "If I Could Knife My Brain," and his outlook more cynical ("Don't talk" he writes in "Koan," "Fart, since by that simpler hole/things are said truer").

While many of his best Vancouver poems were never collected, those that were rank among Acorn's finest: "Words Said Sitting on a Rock Sitting on a Saint," "Poem for Sydney," "I've Gone and Stained With the Colour of Love," and "The Natural History of Elephants," his undisputed masterpiece. He'd written the first draft sitting in Patrick Lane's study, and perfected it, as he often did, through repeated public readings. bissett originally published it in his 1966 "yellow cover" issue of *Blew Ointment*. "That elephant poem," as everyone called it, quickly became a crowd favourite. Simply invoking the first lines—"In the elephant's five-pound brain/The whole world's both table and shithouse"—would send Milton's fans into fits of applause:

> In the elephant's five-pound brain
> The whole world is both table and shithouse
> Where he wanders searching for viands, exchanging great farts
> For compliments. The rumble of his belly
> Is like the contortions of a crumpling planetary system.
> Long has he roved, his tongue longing to press the juices
> Of the ultimate berry, large as
> But tenderer and sweeter than a watermelon;
> And he leaves such signs in his wake such that pygmies have
>   fallen
> And drowned in his great fragrant marshes of turds. . . .

On the surface, it seems an odd poem, but one that's strangely moving and effective. In fact, it's autobiographical, and much of the power comes from emotional truths that electrify the allegory. When Acorn writes, "In the elephant's five-pound brain/ poems are written as a silent substitute for laughter," it's a moment of insight that scrapes at the bone. "The Natural History of Elephants" has a political power as well, which galvanized his young audience. The "official" academic poetry in Canada at the time was turgid; university courses were dominated by American and British poets. But in Acorn there was a Canadian literary figure students could look up to. They knew that before Acorn there was no such thing as a professional poet in this country, and that Milton didn't just create the position, he legitimized it. "The Natural History of Elephants" was a chunk of humanity, as vibrant as the man himself, a poem that—unlike the hyper-intellectual experiments which dominated the little magazines—jumped off the page and demanded to be read out loud. Acorn had gone one better than any of his contemporaries, even Ginsberg. While the Beat poet remains a fine writer to this day, he was never able to top the success of "Howl." Acorn, on the other hand, captured the spirit of one generation in "I Shout Love," then a decade later, he did it again. Not only did "The Natural History of Elephants" become an anthem of Canada's counterculture, it was the best poem Acorn had ever written:

> In the elephant's five-pound brain
> The wind is diverted by the draughts of his breath,
> Rivers are sweet gulps, and the ocean
> After a certain distance is too deep for wading.
> The earth is trivial, it has the shakes
> And must be severely tested, else
> It'll crumble into unstoppable clumps and scatter off
> Leaving the great beast bellowing among the stars. . . .

———

As the decade spun forward, Milton continued to play a leading role in Vancouver's cultural development, helping to establish the alternative magazine *The Georgia Straight*. The idea for a paper first came up in February 1967, when a group of students, poets and radicals got together after a Leonard Cohen reading. They decided that what Vancouver really needed was a "free" press, a newspaper independent from capitalist and imperialist influences, and sent out an invitation to "all those interested in fighting lies/propaganda/terrorism" to meet at writer Rick Kitaeff's house on March 30. Milton was at this meeting, along with thirty others, "a collection of local hippies," most of whom, he claimed in *Cross Canada Writers' Quarterly*, "were sky high on drugs." Out of this second meeting came a blueprint for a "peace paper," soon christened *The Georgia Straight*, a play on the name of the water passage between Vancouver Island and the mainland (a "straight" was the opposite of a hippie, in counterculture parlance; the mainstream media was so offended by this upstart paper that it took to referring to the "Strait of Georgia" in maritime reports).

The first issue of the *Straight* came out on May 5, 1967; Pierre Coupey and one-time *Tish* editor Dan McLeod were listed as coordinating editors, while Milton was named as a contributing editor, along with the likes of writer Stan Persky and Harry Rankin, a well-known communist alderman. Today, Dan McLeod is publisher of the *Straight*; he remembers Milt as being one of the half-dozen people instrumental in getting the paper off the ground. "Milt somehow sold a half-page ad, at a time when we desperately needed the advertising revenue," McLeod says. "He was very energetic and helpful at the start. Just his presence added legitimacy to what we were doing; he was an important figure and that helped to get people to take us seriously." Milton also had a regular column in the paper, and devoted his space in the inaugural issue to the defense of the Advance Mattress coffeehouse against continuing harrassment by local officials. In a leap of logic that only he could have pulled off, Milton linked the plight of the Advanced Mattress to the war in Vietnam. "In Vietnam, a billionaire nation is waging war against a poor and in many ways backward nation," he wrote. "As Kitsilano has the potentiality of becoming converted into a high rise, high rent area—for the greater glory and profit of Free Enterprise—Vietnam has substantial natural resources which could be profitable, so the billionaire nation can become a trillionaire nation."

Milton was now firmly established as a leading light in the Vancouver counterculture, a figure who, like Jack Kerouac in the U.S., was embraced by the hippie generation as their own mad prophet. It was a natural fit. For all their talk of revolution, these new radicals were hard-core Romantics who wanted to reinvent innocence and "get back to the Garden." They sensed in Milton and his misshapen modernism a kindred spirit, a man who created his own counterculture, who'd dropped out before it was fashionable, and provided proof that it was possible to grow up without selling out. But what were the costs? Milton was only forty-four, but two decades of depression, alcohol, bad food, and cheap rooms had taken their toll; he looked ten years older. He was resourceful as ever; one time, he bought a scribbler at Kresge's department store, then spent a couple afternoons in Stanley Park furiously writing down whatever came into his head. He sold the book for $200 to his newly appointed "literary agent," Don MacLeod, owner of a popular used bookstore at the corner of Homer and Pender Streets. MacLeod turned around and sold it for $400 to the University of Alberta, an "authentic" artifact for their CanLit archives. For Milt, the money came in handy; he barely got a couple hundred dollars a month from his disability pension. Typically, he was always on the move from one dingy apartment to another—in a ten-month span he moved from an apartment on Nelson to a basement suite on East Hastings, to a shared house on Granville, to the Parkway Hotel on East Pender—and when he wasn't at the Advance Mattress or *The Georgia Straight* offices at 1666 West 6th Avenue, he was likely hanging out at the Cecil or the Niagara, his two favourite beer parlours. Patrick Lane remembers once finding Milt in the Parkway Hotel; Milt lay in bed, covered in feces, urine and vomit, rambling about Lenin, Marx, Patrick's brother Red, Gwen and her betrayals. It took Lane two hours to clean Milt up, change his clothes, throw his sheets to the alley below: "The shit was stuck to his body—his thighs and his back—and he just lay their crying like a little boy while I cleaned him."

Still, Milton had the fight left in him. Joe Rosenblatt, who'd quit his job with the railroad and moved to Vancouver after getting his first Canada Council writing grant in 1965, recalls Milton's one-man campaign to help a killer whale kept in a cramped tank at the Stanley Park

Aquarium. "Milton harangued the bureaucrats on the parks board, drawing a neat analogy betweeen the whale in her tub and a minnow cramped in a sardine tin," Rosenblatt recalled in "Milton & The Swan," a short memory collected in *The Joe Rosenblatt Reader*. "Months later, the beast blew her mind; she tried to force an exit through a port hole; her massive head was lacerated by splintering glass; immediately the big pool was drained and the big mother was blasted with tranqs and pain killers and sewn up like a football." The whale was never moved to a bigger tank, but she appreciated Milton's efforts on her behalf. "She waved her dorsal right back at me," he told Rosenblatt. "She understood, you know. Those whales could be communists."

While he couldn't save the whale, he was able to help *The Georgia Straight*. In fact, it was doing far better than anyone could have predicted. Its circulation was growing with every issue—and within six months, it had a print run of 60,000. Not only did the magazine offer an alternative source of news and commentary, but people tuned in just for the spicy personal ads: "Horny chick, 20, with baby, wishes to meet young man," read one that ran alongside Acorn's review of a collection of Mao's essays. Another typical ad read, "Two virile males, 19 and 25, looking for two chicks for living companions. Must be sexually inclined and willing to do a little light housework." Meanwhile, the coffeehouse was not faring so well. The problems with city bureaucrats continued. Police and fire officials visited regularly, and hit Gabor Maté and his friends with fine after fine. In early June 1967, an undercover cop was flipping through the selection of alternative papers and underground magazines on sale at the front of the coffeehouse when he came across a radical American paper with a photo of a protest march on the cover. One of the people in the picture was carrying a placard that read "Fuck Hate." For this, the members of the Advance Mattress co-operative were charged and convicted under the Obscenities Act. If the sign had read simply "Hate" there would have been no charge, but, as Maté told me, this was Vancouver in the sixties. "This charge and the court case were the final straws. It takes a lot of effort and energy to keep something like the Advance Mattress going, and all of us were finding ourselves pulled in other directions by this time." The June 28 issue of the *Straight* announced that "due to a remarkable combination of police harassment, vandalism, press hysteria and financial difficulty, the Advance Mattress, Vancouver's only political coffeehouse has been forced to close its doors."

Within months, Milton was having problems at the *Straight* as well. Police harassment and financial difficulties are one thing, but nothing is more disruptive than a little success. With its enormous press runs the *Straight* was quickly becoming something of value, something to be owned—which flew in the face of the founders' original "co-operative" intent. On November 8, Milton got together with Dan McLeod, Pierre Coupey, and Peter Hlookoff to discuss the fate of the paper. Coupey, Hlookoff, and Acorn wanted to keep the co-op, community-based structure, but McLeod wanted to formalize things. He proposed a split ownership, but the others turned him down. Milton's temper got the best of him. He screamed abuse at McLeod, and as he stormed out of the room with Hlookoff and Coupey, he slammed the office door so hard he broke the glass in it. The November 10-23 issue of the *Straight* announced that Acorn, Coupey, Hlookoff and Tony Grinkus had resigned "to form a new (and different) paper." The parentheses were important, since McLeod had moved to legally protect *The Georgia Straight* name.

The former editors dispersed and went on to work with other local alternative papers like the short-lived *The Grape* and *The Western Gate*, but Milton backed off completely. He was losing interest in Vancouver, beginning to "mold," as he told the *Cross Canada Writers' Quarterly*, from "too much moisture in the air." Both Patrick Lane and Joe Rosenblatt say that Milt never felt comfortable on the west coast. The rain didn't help his chronic depression, and he could never get used to just two seasons (wetter and dryer). As the summer of love dissolved into a winter of discontent, Milt began to realize just how far from reality he'd drifted in Vancouver. In his unpublished memoir, he comments on a story he'd told many times during those years, a story that ultimately brought him out of his haze:

> Once I was in a town, I don't know exactly where in Oregon, among mountains near the coast, but on account of the mountains, definitely an inland town. I was having a tight conference

with some fractious characters. The one opposite me—little, red-haired, slightly moustached, and in a blue suit—put his hand inside his coat apparently to draw a gun. My hands were on the table. I didn't tense; relaxed, as a boxer relaxes so's not to bind his muscles; sat with my hands where they were, looking him in the eyes. Not menacing. Menace in such a situation might precipitate the act. During the next long moment he realized I needed only one movement to reach and grasp his wrist; whilst he needed three slower ones to draw and fire. He brought his hand out empty. I told this story for true many times. It was a perfect example of Mao's dictum that you must look for the main contradictions in every situation, not be misled by peripheral appearances. However, one day I got thinking. It couldn't possibly have happened. I'd never been farther south in the States than Seattle, Washington. Then I realized that through most of my years in Vancouver and thereabouts I'd been having a continuing dream, so true to life, so logical I hadn't detected the difference between dream and reality.

After years of desperation, Milton's time spent wandering in the wilderness of Vancouver had come to an end. For one thing, he wanted to spend some time in Charlottetown where both his parents were suffering from poor health; it was doubtful that his father would last much longer. But most of all, Vancouver was too small for a rampaging elephant like Milton Acorn. His friends realized it before he did. In the winter of 1968, Patrick Lane and Joe Rosenblatt packed up Milt's stuff, bought his train ticket, and saw him safely on board, then hung around in the station for a few minutes after the train pulled out, just to make sure he was really gone. Milton Acorn had successfully entered the lion's den, and while he didn't defeat the *Tish* beast, he'd certainly made his presence known. But now the dream was over; Milt was leaving Vancouver and the city would never be the same.

CHAPTER ELEVEN

The Taste of Victory

If this brain's over-tempered
consider that the fire was want
and the hammers were fists . . .
—"I've Tasted My Blood,"
from *Delta*, April 1958

MILTON'S FATHER ROBERT DIED late in September 1968. Milton left no record of how the death affected him (and in fact, no one in the family can remember if Milton was at the funeral). However, we do know that he spent much of the next twelve months wandering, popping up in Dawson Creek, Edmonton, Toronto, Thunder Bay, Ottawa, and Charlottetown—arriving back on The Island in the summer of 1969. While he was travelling, Al Purdy was at work editing a collection of Acorn's poems for the Ryerson Press. Ryerson was *the* poetry publisher in Canada, and this would be the first major collection of his career. "For this volume I cut the number of poems Milton gave me just about in half," Purdy told a reporter from *The Globe & Mail*. "Milton writes a lot of poems but he has a tendency to lose a good number too. He's got a trunkful of them sitting in some CNR express depot. Only, he can't remember in which city." The finished book contained 150 poems culled from *In Love and Anger, Against a League of Liars, The Brain's the Target, Jawbreakers,* the special issue of *The Fiddlehead,* and other magazines, along with two previously unpublished short stories, "The Winged Dingus" and "The Red and Green Pony." The book was called *I've Tasted My Blood;* Ryerson released it in the spring of 1969, while Milton was still on the road.

The reading public that had lost touch with Acorn in the six years since *Jawbreakers* was reintroduced to the depth and range of his talent, and the critics lined up to praise him. John Redmond, in the *Montreal Star,* warned readers that if they didn't buy this book they'd "be committing a mortal sin against Canadian poetry." Robert Weaver, reviewing the book for the *Toronto Star,* called the poems "angry, uptight, sprawling, unexpectedly quiet, sometimes generous, committed for better or worse." George Bowering was impressed, and wrote glowing reviews in the two most influential publications of the time, *The Globe & Mail* and *Canadian Literature.* In *The Globe* review, Bowering said that the collection had convinced him that Acorn was "not only honest and exciting, as no one has ever doubted, but also very much accomplished as an 'artist,' not so much the 'natural' as he has often been pictured." In his introduction to the book, Al Purdy seems to anticipate the critical response, and offers an overview of the poet and his poems, which were by now inseparable entities:

> Acorn speaks from a personal conception of utopian order, as a full citizen of a world that never was and perhaps never will be. All his poems are written from this viewpoint, poems of absolutes, black and white poems: evil is evil and good is good, and never shall the painter's palette or the politician's double tongue turn either to a wishy-washy grey. It's a stance that sometimes appears naïve, occasionally mistaken; but never insincere, always with a voice of power and conviction.
>
> Acorn believes in the perfectibility of people, the infinite capacities and hidden potentials within the individual man—these qualities being inherent and standard equipment with the ordinary person; but not there at all in people who are politically or commercially corrupted.

As I said, it's a black and white universe Acorn inhabits. Most of the time—in fact nearly always—these absolutes lend a power to his work that is foreign to contemporary poets. Acorn himself would say that these other poets don't care enough to take stands, try to change the world, rear up on their hind legs and speak their minds in loud, vulgar and must-be-heard noises.

The early buzz was that Milton was certain to be a Governor General's Award candidate, and no one was surprised when his name appeared on the shortlist. What did raise some eyebrows was that Gwendolyn MacEwen was also listed for her book *The Shadow-Maker*. While no one questioned MacEwen's suitability, many feared how Milton would react. The marriage had effectively ended seven years earlier, and the couple had been officially divorced for three years, but Milt still harboured strong feelings—love *and* hate—for Gwen. He still regularly wrote letters to her, often to simply heap abuse ("For the honour and glory of the capitalist system you undertook to destroy me," he wrote in February 1969). She was so worried about Milt's reaction that she asked Robert Weaver, the senior judge on the awards committee that year, that her book be removed from the shortlist. She reconsidered, though, and finally decided to leave well enough alone. She couldn't spend her life hiding from Milt, afraid that her successes would only cause him anger.

When the awards were announced in the spring of 1970, Milton and his supporters were bitterly disappointed. In an unusual turn of events, the judges awarded two poetry prizes, one to Gwen and one to Milton's west coast rival, George Bowering. Robert Weaver says that he and the other judges, Warren Tallman, and Philip Stratford, were aware that their decision might cause a few ripples. "We knew that there was a lot of support out there for Milt and that there was a strong feeling that this was his best work," Weaver told me in an interview at his Toronto home. "I also think a lot of people felt that there wouldn't be any further work that would live up to this book. I really liked the book as well—all the judges did. And we had no idea that it would cause as big a stir as it did."

Unwittingly, Weaver and company had set up the final battle of the

Great Canadian Poetry War, the conflict that had been brewing since
Tish fired the first insults ten years earlier. But during his five years as
an Awards judge, Weaver was no stranger to controversy. In 1966, his
first year on the committee, the judges selected Margaret Atwood's
The Circle Game for the poetry award, over books by the more estab-
lished poets Margaret Avison, Miriam Waddington and, the sentimen-
tal favourite, Frank Scott. Atwood was only twenty-seven, and up
until that time, the youngest person ever to win a Governor General's
Award. Two years later, there were two scandals. First, the judges
awarded Mordecai Richler for his novel *Cocksure*, which many people
thought was too risqué a work to be selected for honours from the
Queen's Representative. The second was even more embarrassing:
Leonard Cohen declined his award. It was the same year that the
Québécois nationalist writer Hubert Aquin turned down his award for
political reasons, but Cohen's decision was more mysterious. Weaver
recalls a conversation he had with the head of the Governor General's
committee who said "when we listed all the wires and letters and
phone calls we had from Leonard, and we added them up, we decided
that there were more *nos* then *yeses*." The committee took that to mean
Cohen didn't want the award. It didn't, however, stop him from show-
ing up at the party after the awards ceremony. To Weaver's mind
though, the occasional controversy wasn't all that bad. "The Governor
General's Awards people couldn't make up their minds whether they
liked these minor scandals or whether they deplored them. On the one
hand, it was embarrassing to have people do things like what Leonard
Cohen did, but on the other hand, they desperately wanted to get into
the newspapers and on radio and tv, and whenever there was an
uproar of any sort, that helped to give them a higher profile."

After the awards were announced in 1970, a group of poets led by
Joe Rosenblatt and Eli Mandel launched a concentrated attack on the
Governor General's committee. While they were upset that Milton
hadn't won, they were particularly angry that George Bowering had.
To the protestors, who were by and large based in Toronto, Bower-
ing's win was a triumph of the American forces at work in Canadian
culture. It didn't help matters that Warren Tallman was American-
born, and did not hold Canadian citizenship, although he'd lived in

Canada for fourteen years. It also didn't help that Tallman had a direct connection to Bowering, having been advisor on his Master's committee. To the minds of the protestors then, a true Canadian poet had been slighted in favour of a Yankee puppet with friends in high places. To many eyes, the award signaled the Establishment's official sanction, a proclamation that *Tish* had won the Great Canadian Poetry War. But the battle was far from over. An editorial by poets Seymour Mayne and Kenneth Hertz in their Montreal literary magazine *Ingluvin*, sums up the mood of the protestors:

> Either because of literary politics or a gross ignorance of Canadian poetry on the part of the Canada Council jury, Milton Acorn has been denied the Governor General's Award that he truly has earned. Milton Acorn has been an individual and productive figure in Canadian poetry for over fifteen years. Over those years he has built up a solid body of work characterized by excellence and by social and political concerns largely absent in most Canadian writing. He was certainly never a literary careerist gathering up his collection of approving pats from the poetic and academic bureaucracy. He maintained his independence and forged one of the few true voices in Canadian poetry.
>
> The fact that Milton Acorn was denied the award may be symptomatic of what is happening generally in poetry in Canada. Increasing preoccupation with American styles and concerns, and neglect of the Canadian traditions are obfuscating our past. Since the thirties such figures as Scott, Birney, Livesay, Klein, Layton, Souster, Page, Dudek and Purdy have created a Canadian idiom—a source from which younger poets could forge their own language and locus. Now we have Americans heading our English Departments, editing our literary magazines, anthologizing our young poets, and even passing judgements on our own poets for our national awards.

There may have been another, more practical reason why the protestors focused their attack on Warren Tallman. Because of his nationality and his connection to Bowering he was the most vulnerable. But

what about Robert Weaver? He was the senior judge, and, theoreti-
cally, had the most influence on the committee's decision. But of
course, the protestors couldn't attack Weaver. First of all, Canadian
literature had no greater champion. Through his work with *The
Tamarack Review* , which he co-founded in 1956, and CBC Radio shows
like *Anthology*, Weaver provided ongoing forums for writers and al-
most single-handedly saved the short story from extinction in Canada.
Secondly, while Weaver was widely regarded as easy-going and fair-
minded, he did have a lot of power, and few writers wanted to take a
chance on alienating him. In any case, while Weaver understood the
sentiment behind the protest, he didn't follow the logic of the national-
ists. Their complaint was that Bowering had turned his back on Cana-
dian poetics and wrote in the American idiom. But Weaver didn't see
that much difference between Bowering and Acorn. "Both of them
were influenced by Charles Olson and the Black Mountain school,"
Weaver says. "In fact, there were more similarities between Acorn and
Bowering than there were between either of them and Gwen. She was
a much more exotic poet."

For his part, George Bowering tried to take the criticism in stride.
However, he couldn't help but think that there was more going on.
"I've never been able to swallow the notion that Milton's animosity was
because of me getting the award," Bowering told me. "I think he had
some strong feeling about Gwen getting it as well. He just didn't feel
that he could go after Gwen in public." He also actively endorsed
Milton's book, writing two important reviews designed—as Bowering
later explained in the Winter/Spring 1972/73 issue of *Blackfish*—to
make it "known among the Eastern literary establishment that I
thought that their man, Acorn, should get the prize."

————

Acorn had lost the big battle, but the war wasn't over yet. Rosenblatt
and Mandel took up the fight, forming a committee of poets to organ-
ize the Canadian Poets' Award, a kind of anti-Governor General's
Award. Mandel, a professor at York University and a Governor Gen-
eral's poetry award winner in 1967, spearheaded the letter-writing

campaign, enlisting the endorsement of Irving Layton, perhaps the most famous poet in the country. Layton jumped on board, telling the press that Milton had more talent in his little finger than Bowering had in his entire body, and criticized the Governor General's committee for not granting him the award in the first place. "It's a great blow to the man," Layton said. "Milton has suffered in mental health, physical health and poverty. That kind of courage should be recognized. Here is a genuine poet, one who hasn't gone through the academic mill, which is where reputations are being made these days—a genuine poet as so many in academia are not." Mandel circulated an appeal, co-signed by Layton, explaining the project:

> We wish to register our protest that the Governor General's Awards Committee failed to include Milton Acorn's distin-guished collection of poems *I've Tasted My Blood* among the win-ners of the Literary Awards this year. We want to indicate to Milton that we admire and applaud his work; and we want to honor him for his contribution to Canadian poetry. We propose, then, that a fund be raised and presented to Milton Acorn as the Canadian Poet's Award. You are invited to contribute whatever amount you feel appropriate. Please send the money or pledge of money as soon as possible.

The "People's Poet Award," as it came to be called, quickly became a *cause célèbre* in literary circles, and for once, Milton was in the right place at the right time. A wave of nationalism had been rising as Canada approached its centennial, and for a few years afterwards, Canadian artists and intellectuals felt that their country might be freed from outside dominance, or rather, that with enough presence of mind, Canada could be truly autonomous if only Canadians would grab the opportunity. It was this independent spirit that helped sweep Pierre Trudeau to power in 1968. With the Governor General's Award controversy, Milton became an ideal symbol of both the fears and expectations of Canadian nationalists. Of course, there's also the matter that *I've Tasted My Blood* was a great book, a collection of the finest poems by one of Canada's greatest poets. Within it, Acorn encom-

passed the entire range of Canadian poetic experience; lyrics and son-
nets that harkened back to the Song Fishermen and Archibald
Lampman through to experimental masterpieces like "I Shout Love"
and "The Natural History of Elephants." For a country in constant
search for an identity, here was one of the finest expressions of its
poetic voice.

Within a few days of announcing the award, the organizers had
received dozens of donations from people like Earle Birney, Leonard
Cohen, Douglas Fetherling, and John Glassco. Layton even hit up the
Premier of P.E.I., Alexander Bradshaw Campbell, for a $200 donation,
which rounded out the award prize money at $1,000, not bad consider-
ing that in those days the actual Governor General's Award winner
only got $2,500. The renegade poets organized a presentation cere-
mony at Grossman's Tavern on Spadina Avenue, Milt's favourite pub,
and sent out invitations to everyone who was anyone in Canadian
literature excluding, of course, the Governor General:

> You are invited to salute
> Milton Acorn
> the People's Poet,
> at Grossman's Tavern
> 79 Spadina Avenue, Toronto
> on Saturday, May 16th
> from 7:30 p.m. till midnight
> for the presentation of
> The Canadian Poet's Award
> created this year to honor
> Milton Acorn's book
> I'VE TASTED MY BLOOD,
> CASH BAR AND FOOD.

Early Saturday night a strange mix of literati and illiterati began to
show up at Grossman's smoky beer hall. Irving Layton, Al Purdy and

Joe Rosenblatt were there, friends from Milt's past, as was Margaret Atwood—all in all, a dozen past and future Governor General's Award winners made their way to Grossman's Tavern to sit shoulder to shoulder with the regulars—the career drunks and castaways—and celebrated guests like "Honest" Ed Mirvish, when he was just owner of a discount store and had yet to begin his theatre empire.

On the way down to the tavern, Purdy had got a funny idea. He called up Robert Weaver and invited him to join in the festivities. Weaver politely declined, fearing that either Milt would hit him —which would have been unpleasant—or, after a suitable number of beers, Milt would get sentimental and attempt a public reconciliation—which would have been worse. At 8 p.m., after the tabletops and floors were slick with beer, the shabby poet shuffled and swaggered his way to the makeshift podium to accept his award. Cameras whirred and flashbulbs flashed. It was a media event. But many of the poet's old friends were surprised by Milt's appearance. They hadn't seen him since he left for Vancouver eight years earlier; he looked like he'd aged a lifetime. Was he smaller? He was certainly stooped over slightly, and seemed to have trouble walking. His face was lined and creased, his fingers bent, and although he wore a heavy wool suit and had his hair nicely trimmed, he had an air of disorder about him. His laughter was like a sort of curse, his big, big smile, a wince. Eli Mandel made the presentation. He handed Milt a cheque for $1,000, and slipped the trophy, a saucer-sized, silver-grey medallion on purple velvet ribbon, around Milt's neck. On one side of the medal was the inscription *Canadian Poets' Award 1970, I've Tasted My Blood*. On the other, the grammatically incorrect *Milton Acorn, The Peoples' Poet*. As Milt stood there beaming, Mandel raised his fist and shouted "Power to the people!" The crowd cheered. Milt was once again shy. Speechless.

In the midst of the cheers and the slow motion applause of beer bottles landing on table-tops, Milton Acorn took a deep breath. Perhaps he was overwhelmed. This was, after all, one of the most astounding moments in the history of Canadian Literature, the climax of the Great Canadian Poetry War. All at once, Milt scowled. "I'm out of this world —" he shouted. He had their attention:

— I'm in
Either here or in the mirror on the wall
For my curious critical drinking eyes;
For you in this neat book or the clang of vibrations in sight,
    in sound;
By this blade stamped and honed I decree
I shall be another man to you, my description confounded. . . .

He had started writing "On Shaving Off His Beard" back in Van-
couver, and after dozens of re-writes, finished a few days before the
ceremony. In his postscript to the only published version of the poem
(which was quickly shelved after the Village Bookstore Press realized
they'd bound the pages out of order), Acorn called it an "experimental
poem," an attempt to discover what would happen if he "deliberately
descended into a vulgar, brawling tone, like a drunk standing in a bar
and yelling for a fight":

If I could stand off from myself
In a thoughtful haze called the soul of the world
And watch myself without myself being aware,
Not every motion flatteringly rehearsed and studied as it is
    in a mirror,
I might not even like myself, or actually be too awed
For like or dislike: but then the razor and its blade
Are also poised, also studied—reflected in the mirror. . . .

He read the complete poem, which took almost twenty minutes,
then launched into a new, expanded version of "I Shout Love," and by
the end the crowd was standing, ready to weep, ready to roar, ready to
tear apart any money-plated bastard foolish enough to stumble into the
tavern—Honest Ed excepted. The rest of the night belonged to Milt.
He wandered the tavern, old friends and new admiring his medal,
slapping him on the back, buying him beers. He misplaced the cheque,
twice, and finally lost it for good, somehow, under a pile of coats and
chairs at the back of the room. Eventually the janitor, who could have
used a G-note himself, found it and brought it back to him. Milton's

triumph was complete. "I've always written my poems to the people," he told Kaspars Dzeguze of *The Globe & Mail*. "So I appreciate most receiving the award as the People's Poet." Around midnight, the old warrior made his way to the washroom. He hunched over a sink and turned the water on, letting it run through his fingers for a moment. The People had spoken. The true poets had risen in defiance of the establishment and annointed him victor of the Poetry Wars. Milt splashed his face with water and rubbed the back of his neck as tears streamed down his cheeks.

CHAPTER TWELVE

The People's Poet

I'll be a statue to myself. Cigar stuck out
Like the smooth broken-off stump of a dead limb.
—"I'll Be a Statue to Myself," from
More Poems for People

THE PEOPLE HAD SPOKEN, and soon the people would be listening.

By June of 1970 Milton had taken up permanent residence at the Waverley Hotel, on Spadina near College, in the heart of a run-down area that had once been Toronto's garment district. It was a deliberate choice. The area had strong working-class ties—in the forties, it had sent a communist to the Ontario legislature—and was now home to derelicts and down-and-out drunks. Two doors down was the Scott Mission, an outreach for street people, and conveniently located downstairs was the Silver Dollar Pub, where Milt passed many afternoons and evenings drinking beer and espousing his views on the exploitation of the masses as the strippers did their thing fifteen feet away. He lived and worked in a $20-a-week room, half-buried in a litter of books and papers on the floor, a giant hammer and sickle decorating the wall above his bed. Ensconced in his proletarian surroundings, he set to work on a new book of poems which he intended to be the definitive statement of purpose for the People's Poet. No more editors telling him to tone down his politics. He would write working-class poems in the Canadian vernacular, no matter what the consequence. He'd already chosen a title, *More Poems for People*, borrowed from Dorothy's 1947 Governor General's Award-winning *Poems for People*. Milton saw Livesay as part of a Canadian poetic continuum that stretched back in time through Joe Wallace and Archibald Lampman. These poets belonged to what Milton called a "People's Poet" tradition, which, according to Milton's friend and editor James Deahl, could be characterized by the following "rules":

> A poetry that believes in people and the basic *goodness* of people; that believes in the perfectability of people *within* history; that believes in the social and *spiritual* progress; that believes that a poet must be sincere, truthful, direct in the use of language, and highly moral; that is democratic, written *for* people, and does not require special knowledge on the part of the reader; that venerates nature and the natural world; that is socially engaged, opposing racism, sexism, and other forms of discrimination; and is written by poets who truly *like* people.

Around the same time, Milton began increasing his efforts to bring his poems directly to the people. Shortly after winning his People's Poet Medal, Milt met a radical actor-musician named Cedric Smith. Smith, who today is best-known as Alec King from CBC Television's *Road to Avonlea*, was planning a series of midnight concerts at Toronto Workshop Production when the technical manager of this alternative theatre introduced him to Milt. Smith thought the senior poet would be a perfect addition to his concert troupe, so he talked Milt into joining up. Milt shared Smith's love of theatrics, and used his shabby appearance to his benefit. "We did the first half of the show without Milt," Smith recalled. "We had this couch on stage, and during the intermission, Milt would wander out on stage, sit on the couch and read the newspaper. I got this idea because when I'd met Milt at Grossman's, he'd been sitting there with *The Globe & Mail*, expounding and elaborating on the day's news. So Milt would sit there, reading away, and everybody thinking he was the janitor, and I give him the cue for him to recite some of his poems."

While the midnight shows didn't break any box office records—Cedric remembers nights with forty people in the audience—they did have an impact. The performers came to call themselves Perth County Conspiracy (Does Not Exist), and signed a recording deal with Columbia Records, becoming the first "hippie" band in the country to get a contract with a major label. With three singer-songwriters (Smith, Richard Keelan and Terry Jones), the band had a sound vaguely reminiscent of Crosby, Stills and Nash—but with the kind of genuine left-wing political commitment no American band would dare to embrace. (Their 1976 album *PCC Kanada* was recorded and mixed in East Berlin "for distribution in socialist countries.") Columbia released their first album in 1970, the self-titled *Perth County Conspiracy (Does Not Exist)*. Their next album, 1971's *Perth County Conspiracy Alive*, was recorded live at the Bathurst Street United Church, and featured a photo of a topless, potbellied Milt on its inside cover. Smith had set to music Acorn's "I Spun You Out" (from 1963's *The Fiddlehead* special) and included it on the album. Smith would go on to set several more of his poems to music—including "I Shout Love," "You Growing," and "Martyrs," an obscure poem published in *New Frontiers*—and the poet would often appear with the band in concert, reciting works like "The Natural History of Elephants" as drums pounded an African rhythm in the background. In any case, Acorn's work with Perth County introduced him to an even broader audience, and a genuine context for him to develop and expand his voice.

In the spring of 1971 the People's Poet found the perfect publisher for his People's Poems. NC Press—the initials stood for "New Canada"—was a publishing arm of the Canadian Liberation Movement, a communist organization that was nationalist and decidedly anti-American. One day, Milton wandered into the CLM office on College Street, half a block away from the Waverley. He joined on the spot, quickly becoming one of its most vocal and visible supporters. The CLM was headed by Gary Perly, who was then a theoretical leftist, and today runs the family business, Perly Maps of Toronto. Perly and his group believed in a "scientific connection" between socialism and patriotism, and called for the Canadian working class to rise up and revolt against Yankee Imperialism. According to a blurb for the CLM:

> Canada is a colony. Our trade unions, our natural resources, our culture, our universities, and our industry—all are controlled from across the border, the longest undefended border in the world, which we share with the largest imperialist power in the world. There are those who, seeing the extent of the colonialism, believe the battle to be lost. We do not see it that way. We see people across the country rising up against U.S. imperialism: workers struggling to forge militant, democratic Canadian unions, farmers fighting U.S. agribusiness, students opposing the takeover of the universities by increasing numbers of American professors. To end our exploitation, to build a new Canada where people hold the real power, we must unite patriotic and progressive Canadians in a fighting organization dedicated to the achievement of independence and socialism.

While this mix of Marxism and nationalism might seem strange, flying in the face of the Communist International, it wasn't out of place in the spirit of the times. A wave of nationalism had swept the country following the Centennial, and at every level of government and culture, Canadians were struggling to assert control over their country.

Chris Faiers was one of the young people who turned to the CLM. He was a Canadian who'd grown up in the U.S., then moved to Britain in the late sixties to live on a commune. He returned to Canada in the early 1970s, and enrolled at the University of Guelph. It's there that Faiers was recruited by the CLM. At first, he believed he simply joined something called the 85% Committee, a CLM front group promoting a "home grown" quota for professors at Canadian universities. Once Faiers proved that he could be trusted, Perly asked him to join the CLM proper. The mystery surrounding the CLM was part of its appeal. "A lot of us were disaffected hippies," Faiers recalled in a telephone interview from his home in Marmora, in rural Ontario. "We were desperately looking for meaning in our lives. And then here was this answer. You could join the CLM and the answers were all laid out for you." Accord-

ing to Faiers, Milton was an important figure who lent the CLM credi-
bility. "Milton was the main cultural representative that we could pre-
sent to the public. He was the perfect manifestation of all this stuff,
because he was a Maoist and Stalinist, and yet he was strongly Cana-
dian. He embodied the movement." Faiers says that Milton, however,
stayed out of the day-to-day operation of the organization; he was no
longer interested in political power. He was content in his role as
unofficial cultural attaché and in lending his input to the secret Stalin-
ist cell which ran the CLM. Besides, he had enough to worry about. The
People's Poet Medal was weighing heavy around his neck. "Being the
poet's poet is something I have to live with," Milton told a CBC Radio
interviewer at the time. "Being the People's Poet is something I have to
justify." He worked hard on his new collection, but the poems came
slowly and only after countless rewrites. True, he was putting pressure
on himself to live up to an imaginary standard, but he was also having
a hard time finding his voice. He felt that it was time to construct a
distinctly Canadian language as "intercomprehensible," as he wrote in
the Winter/Spring 1972/73 *Blackfish*, "with English, Scots and Ameri-
can as most Slavic languages are intercomprehensible." Acorn believed
that he spoke this language, and his growing success performing with
Perth County Conspiracy proved it was effective. But he struggled to
translate it to the printed page. He finally finished *More Poems for
People* in the spring of 1972, the first collection of new poems he'd
produced in a decade. On the surface, *More Poems for People* seemed
very much a period piece. There's a homemade feel to the book, right
down to the hasty cover portrait drawn by Greg Curnoe. Acorn also
seems to have fallen under the *Tish* spell; there's a lot of postmodern
experiments with form, like these lines from "Hey You Guevara":

> Hey
>   *YOU*
>   Guevara
>   !!!!!!!!!!!!!!!!!!!!!!!!?

However, *More Poems for People* was the most political book of
Acorn's career; virtually every poem can be read as a denunciation of

capitalism and imperialism, and a celebration of the common Canadian. In fact Milton found a way to turn the process of publishing itself into a revolutionary act. Always one to put his money where his mouth was—and taking a cue from socialist folk singers of the 1950s—Milton declared that the poems could "be used free of charge by anyone serving the cause of Canadian Independence and the cause of the working people in any country." There is an odd energy to the book and an evenness of tone that makes it the most consistent collection of Acorn's career. But were they good poems? On my first reading, I couldn't tell. Something was lacking. Then Cedric Smith pointed out that the poems came to life when read out loud. "There's a natural rhythm and music to them," Smith said. "You don't see that when you look at them on the page; they're meant to be spoken." Milton's experiments were an effort to recreate on the page an accurate "reading" of the poems. He'd come full circle, bringing the Canadian poetry world with him. Incorporating elements of social realism, modernism and postmodernism, he reinvented populist poetry and reinstated the oral tradition, a literate, literary Joe Wallace speaking to every day Canadians in their own voice. And that voice was heard.

While reviews of *More Poems for People* were mixed, the public response was phenomenal. According to James Deahl, the book sold 10,000 copies, making it one of the top-selling Canadian poetry books of all time. The Great Canadian Poetry War had propelled Milton into the public eye, and his readings now drew hundreds of people. The People's Poet was as much an entertainer as a literary figure. His fans—and make no mistake about it, Acorn had fans—came to see the onstage antics of the mythic socialist-carpenter-poet who, rumour had it, had a steel plate in his head courtesy of a German submarine attack during World War II. When Milton recited "I Shout Love" or "The Natural History of Elephants," or poems from the new book like "Ode to the Timothy Eaton Memorial," the room echoed with the voices of the many fans who'd set the poems to memory. "I've never seen anything like it, before or since," said Chris Faiers, who organized several of Milt's readings for the CLM. Faiers had been to poetry recitals in England, all staid, boring, and poorly attended, and wasn't prepared for the populist poetry scene in Canada. "Milt was like a rock star,"

Faiers recalled. "People would applaud and scream and buy his books; they'd line up hours before we'd open the doors, just to get a seat near Milt." It was the start of what proved to be the Golden Age of Canadian Poetry, when poets had a ready audience and a government willing to fund their work. And there, at the very centre, speaking in the ancient voice of the Canadian people, was Milton Acorn, whose every public appearance was proof he'd realized the goal he'd first conceived twenty years earlier in a dingy Montreal apartment when he swore that if poetry was not already a profession, he would damn well make it one.

CHAPTER THIRTEEN

The Elephant's Graveyard

In the elephant's five-pound brain
Death is accorded no belief and old friends
Are continually expected, patience
Is longer than the lives of glaciers and the centuries
Are rattled like toy drums. A life is planned
Like a brush-stroke on the canvas of eternity,
And the beginning of a damnation is handled
With great thought as to its middle and its end.
        —"The Natural History of Elephants,"
            from *I've Tasted My Blood*

Charlottetown, Prince Edward Island, July 1986

A RAVEN CALLED. THEN ANOTHER.

The first light of dawn lifted in the distance, and although Charlottetown's shops hid the horizon, the birds knew that a new day had begun. An old man asleep on a park bench was awakened by the ravens' song. He listened for a moment, then brought his hand to his mouth and replied, "Kee-ah!" Sometimes he felt that he was the last man on earth who could speak to the birds.

Milton Acorn sat up. He looked like a bum. His clothes—a red and black flannel work shirt and jeans—were worn, and hung loosely, suggesting that once, someone greater wore them. His age was impossible to guess—perhaps as young as fifty, and maybe as much as seventy-five, for he was not the kind of man who had weathered well. His cheeks were gaunt, gutted, his eyes yellow and sunken, his thin beard stained brown in patches from the cigars he smoked—*Bances Habana Corona*, at seventy-two cents a pop—which were, along with the well-used silk handkerchiefs, his only extravagances. But there was a gentleness in Milton's movements; a kind of elephantine grace, a ponderous, cautious awareness behind every motion. He began to cough, a deep, dry death bark that built until he was breathless. The ravens took off, circled Confederation Square, eyeing this old bird with his strange call, until they lit again in another oak, further away.

———

Milton had moved back to The Island in 1982, after ten years in Toronto. He'd become a fixture in Hogtown's streets and bars, and as his emotional and physical health declined, he drifted into self-parody. But the people still came to his readings, and the Literary Establishment was finally granting him his due. In 1975 he was awarded the Governor General's Award for *The Island Means Minago*, an experimental collection of old and new poems, essays, dramatic excerpts, prose fragments and photographs which had been rescued from the garbage by one of Milt's editors at NC Press. For the ceremony, Milt bought a $300 suit from Tip Top Tailors, and wore his best pair of runners (not, he later explained, out of irreverence, but because his corns were acting up). In his jacket pocket he carried his treasured People's Poet Award, and as he accepted his specially-bound copy of *The Island Means Minago* from Jules Léger, his aging mother looked on with pride.

Two years later, Milton had a play produced (*The Road to Charlottetown*, about the P.E.I. tenant rebellions of the 1800s, co-written by Cedric Smith) and a new book, *Jackpine Sonnets*. Published by Steel Rail Publishing, which was created when the Canadian Liberation Movement imploded, the book represented Acorn's struggle to create a distinctly Canadian poetic form. He took the fourteen lines and regular rhyme patterns of the classic sonnet, and, keeping the rhetorical element of the sonnet intact (Acorn recognized that at its heart—"How do I love thee? Shall I compare you to a summer's day?"—the sonnet was a poetic argument), he combined it with the free-flowing form and content of Modernist poetry. The result was a free-form sonnet, with lines, metre and length determined not by an arbitrary rule, but by the organic demands of the content. To Acorn's mind, this unassuming and highly adaptive sonnet was a perfect reflection of the Canadian character. "I have named it after one of my favorite trees—the Jackpine, which can grow in any earth in which you plant it, so long as it's not crowded," Acorn wrote in his introduction to the book. *"If it looks like nothing on earth, not even a Jackpine, it must be a Jackpine . . . or a Canadian."* But by now, the reading public was already forgetting Acorn. The book received lukewarm reviews, and sold poorly. His invention, the jackpine sonnet, never caught on.

In May of that year, the University of Prince Edward Island granted Milton an honourary law degree. He was thrilled with the award and delighted to discover that former Prime Minister John Diefenbaker was a co-recipient. Dief was a staunch nationalist and renowned Red Tory, which made him all right in Milt's books. "One hundred years from now," Milt said after the ceremony with a gleam in his eye, "people will be saying, Diefenbaker? Diefenbaker? Oh yes, he's the fellow who got his honourary degree along with Milton Acorn." From that day on, the poet introduced himself as Dr. Milton Acorn.

For the next five years he continued to write and teach and perform public readings, although by now his health problems were insurmountable. Many people—too many—remember only a broken man, obsessed by thoughts of Zulu warriors, an ardent anti-abortionist ("it is so utterly against the spirit of Marx," he'd complain), a man who stood up at the Annual General Meeting of the League of Canadian Poets in the spring of 1981 to relentlessly attack a motion supporting gay rights, until an exasperated Joe Rosenblatt called him a "Nazi" and told him to "sit down and shut up." Someone had to lead Milton away by the hand. He shouted all the way out the doors, and on. The League could go to hell, he told himself. He was done with Toronto, done with the

endless b.s. and conspiracies and gossips and petty jealousies, all aimed
to bring him down. His work was done; he'd achieved everything he'd
set out to do—except find a wife, of course, but there was still time for
that. Time. That time was a commodity in short supply. Thirty years
ago—was it really thirty years?—he left the Island to find his fame and
fortune. Perhaps he hadn't made his fortune, but the fame was there in
spades. Now it was time to return to his Island. It was time to go home
and prepare to die.

———

Even after his return to The Island Acorn wasn't finished. In 1982
Ragweed Press published his uneven yet compelling sonnet cycle *Captain Neal MacDougal & The Naked Goddess*—with many of the poems
"dictated" to Milt by the spirit of the Captain himself. A year later,
McClelland & Stewart released *Dig Up My Heart: Selected Poems, 1952-1983* as part of its prestigious New Canadian Poets series, introducing
Milton's best work to a new generation of Canadian readers. These
selected poems remain in print thirteen years later, an impressive
achievement. Acorn also began three other books during his final
years—*The Uncollected Acorn*, two sets of jackpine sonnets, *Whiskey
Jack*, and *A Stand of Jackpine*, with James Deahl—none of which were
published until after his death.

Acorn spent the remainder of his days a national legend and a local
curiosity, the kind of crazy eccentric that most people would cross the
street to avoid. Although he gave up the booze and the pills, substituting them with vitamins and health food concoctions, his health continued to falter. In the spring of 1984, his mother passed away.

But Milt pressed on.

———

Milton stood and stretched like a cat, then bent forward to touch his
toes. He barely got past his thighs. Then he tried a couple deep knee
bends, but the cool night air had got to his joints. He swung his arms
vigorously—that would get the old blood flowing—then boxed with a

worthy oak branch. Once, he'd been quite a fighter. Not a good fighter, mind you. In fact, he'd tell you, he was the worst fighter you'd ever seen. Milton checked his watch. The Parkside Pharmacy wouldn't open for another two hours, and he would have to wait to replenish his stock of vitamins. In the old days he drank wine just to make it through the day, but now it was nothing stronger than black coffee—no cream because of his heart, no sugar because of the diabetes—and he ate vitamins by the handful in hopes that he would make it through another year. B-12 for vigor. C to boost the immune system. E for the heart. A to keep the cancer that had crept into his lungs at bay.

Milton set off to find himself a coffee. Down the block a man in a suit and tie strode toward him, already on his way to the office. He looked familiar; perhaps they'd been schoolmates? "The early bird catches the worm," Milton called out, with a mad smile. The man in the suit crossed the street. That happened a lot to Milton, for it seemed that all his life people would go out of their way to get out of his way. He liked to call himself "The People's Poet," but in fact most people were afraid of him, or just flat out didn't like him, and certainly didn't understand him. Milton picked up his torn notebook, and thought back to an indifferent May night back in 1970 when, in a smoky beer hall off Toronto's Spadina Avenue, they'd met to honour him, presenting him with his People's Poet Medal. Milt had hung onto the medal for the next fourteen years, wearing it proudly whenever the occasion warranted, which was practically all the time. He lost it, of course. Eventually, he lost everything.

But not The Island. He'd left The Island years ago, that was true, but The Island had never left him. And now Charlottetown was The Elephant's Graveyard, and the elephant had returned to die.

A raven cried; the sky was crimson and ready for morning. After coffee, he'd take a City Cab to visit his sister Mary Hooper and her family, just outside of town. Then maybe later he'd head back into town and check out things at Patrick's Rose and Grey Room. But first, he was content to be alone, to listen to the ravens gripe about the quality of grubs, and contemplate the beginning, middle and end of his own particular damnation.

CHAPTER FOURTEEN

Final Passage

> . . . if you're inclined to feel sympathetic
> Towards the horse-player—don't—the synthetic
> World that he lived in hung less upon earnings
> Than on his justification. The spurnings
> Of him by the fates inflated his ego;
> For since he was markedly luckless then, ergo,
> the world was conferring on him the distinction
> of arranging affairs to effect his extinction!
> A silly idea, I'll grant, but it saved him
> From feeling the cog in the grind that enslaved him. . . .
> —"Grey Girl's Gallop," *New*
> *Frontiers*, Winter 1955

IN MAY 1986, MILTON GAVE A READING with James Deahl at Grossman's Tavern in Toronto, the scene of his greatest triumph, the People's Poet award ceremony. Two hours later, Milton suffered a heart attack. After release from hospital, he returned to Prince Edward Island, although he never fully regained his health. In July, he was dealt another blow when his youngest sister Helen succumbed to cancer. Over the next three months, he was in and out of the Queen Elizabeth

Hospital. Finally, on August 20, 1986, the Great Marxist called for an Anglican priest. Milton renounced his Godless ways and accepted Jesus Christ as his personal Saviour. A little while later, he let out a mighty groan that shook the hallways of the hospital. It was finished. Milton Acorn was dead.

The funeral was held at St. Peter's Cathedral church, then Milton was interred in the family plot at St. Peter's Anglican Cemetery, along-side his mother, father, and sister. Richard Lemm, a fellow Islander and president of the League of Canadian Poets, and Libby Oughton of Ragweed Press read a few of Milt's poems; then, to the sound of bagpipes, Milt was laid to rest. Legend has it that Milt died alone and forgotten, and that his death went unnoticed across the country, but nothing could be further from the truth. Newspapers, magazines and television ran obituaries and tributes. In Toronto, a group of poets got together and put on a wake. Disappointed with the turnout, they formed a committee and planned a bigger, better wake. The commit-tee was chaired by Bob Kell, the artist who drew the cover of *Jackpine Sonnets*, and included Joyce Wayne, Milt's editor at Steel Rail, Cedric Smith, Don Cullen (from the Embassy days), Chris Faiers, James Deahl, and writer Rick Salutin. The wake committee met every Wednesday night for almost a year, planning and arguing; at times tensions ran high, but the committee managed to pull it off.

The wake began in the afternoon at Grossman's Tavern, hosted by Deahl, where Chris Faiers was awarded the Milton Acorn Memorial Poetry Award. In the evening, the wake continued at Toronto's Thea-tre Passe Muraille, with Cedric Smith hosting and fronting a band that included Loreena McKennitt. Purdy read "House Guest" and remi-nisced about the old days in Montreal. Patrick Lane read too, along with a half dozen others, but the best line of the night was delivered by Milt's sister Mary Hooper. "You want stories of Milton when he was a little boy, but I can't remember Milton ever being a little boy," she said. "He was a little old man, that is, until he became a poet, and then he was a little boy." The most touching moment came courtesy of Gwen MacEwen. Time had not been kind to her, and although she was now recognized as one of the major poets of her era, she'd sunk into her own personal abyss of alcoholism and depression. When she took the stage of the Theatre Passe Muraille the audience hushed. Her face was bloated, her eyes sunken and shadowed; she had barely a year left to live. Gwen smiled, then began to recite—from memory—"You Growing," a poem Milton had written in the beach house on Ward's Island, during their brief marriage:

> You growing and your thoughts threading
> the delicate strength of your focus,
> out of clamour of voices,
> demanding faces and noises,
> apart from me but vivid
> as when I kissed you and chuckled:
>
> Wherever you are be fearless;
> And wherever I am I hope to know
> you're moving vivid beyond me,
> so I grow by the strength
> of your fighting for your self, your life.

————

Today, Milton Acorn is largely forgotten. While his artistic legacy is rich—more than one thousand of his poems have survived, and there may be a thousand more lost or discarded—many people only remember the troubled and troubling eccentric, the broken man consumed by rage and sorrow. "Acorn's insistence on the importance of his polemic verse has undoubtedly impaired the appreciation of his poetry," wrote former *Tish* editor Frank Davey, in *From There To Here*, his useful guide to contemporary Canadian literature. "His lyrics, his portraits of workers and various experimental poems . . . have been overlooked by teachers and anthologists distracted by the public image he has created. His criticism and public statements have alienated a number of anthologists and fellow writers." True. But what these detractors forget is that he wrote some of the finest verse this country has ever seen. Poet after poet I interviewed praised Milton's poetry, and most agreed that while he published many inferior poems, particularly in the latter stages of his life, his best dozen (two dozen? hundred?) stack up against anything else in Canadian literature. Al Purdy, for one, believes that eventually Acorn will get his due, and that his old friend is only a victim of the times.

"There is not a high opinion of Maritime poets in general in this country," Purdy says. "And he worked outside of the academic world, which is where most reputations are made and broken. Also, Acorn was crude. He was argumentative, verbally abusive, and always spoke his mind. He was an individual in just about every way you could think of, and maybe that hurts him too, because in Canada we want our poets to be nice and pleasant and polite. And then of course, he bought into the jargon of the communists. Dialectical materialism? What the hell is that? His politics, his personality—just about everything about him—rubbed people the wrong way. But a poet should be measured by his best work, and on that count, Milt can hold his own with anybody."

Joe Rosenblatt agrees. Despite their falling out, Rosenblatt maintains that Acorn was a powerful presence in Canadian literature. "He was a superb poet on many, many levels. He also wrote some terrible stuff too, and the terrible stuff was influenced by his political didacticism. The trouble is, you start writing about a politician—politicians die. But trees don't, fish don't, fishermen don't. Why has Blake's 'Tyger' lasted for centuries? Why? Because it's a timeless thing. Milton wrote some timeless poems. And so what if he alienated a lot of people? We're not running a feel-good agency; this is not a group therapy session. He could be a schmuck, but that had absolutely nothing to do with his writing. The task of the poet is to write memorable poetry. Everything else will look after itself."

Rosenblatt wonders if Acorn's dilemma is not indicative of the problem facing all Canadian poets today. We live in a country where sales of 500 copies of a poetry book would be considered a bestseller, where poetry, once the heartbeat of the nation, is completely removed from everyday life. "I don't think there's a visceral need for poets here," Rosenblatt says. "In Ireland, there is a great tradition of poetry. You go to pubs, and people quote you a poem; you go to Scotland, they'll talk about Robbie Burns—they'll commit his poems to memory.

You can't say the same thing about Canada. You go into a pub in Canada, they talk about Wayne Gretzky. Should we mad off about that? No. I just think that this is in many a young country. Maybe we just need to grow up a little more, and accept and understand that we have our own tradition and our own culture."

Still, there are signs that things are changing. Since 1987, his home town of Charlottetown has hosted the National Milton Acorn Festival. It's grown every year, presenting poetry, music, storytelling and theatre—and is now one of the largest of its kind in the country. His few available books continue to sell, while many of his out-of-print titles have become collectors' items: a signed, mint-condition copy of *In Love and Anger,* a book Milton couldn't give away, is today worth $1,000 to a serious collector. Meanwhile, his own brand of poetry—a strange combination of the ancient, the Romantic, the modern, and postmodern, the oral and the literary—prefigures today's spoken-word poetry revival. "For a person destined to be a natural man, I was born at a bad time, for Nature was just going out of fashion," Milton Acorn once said. But I disagree. He was a man for all ages, and for none, a man who lived with his feet firmly planted in one world—the world of flop-houses and sickness and poverty and madness—while his eyes were forever trained on something brighter, something magnificent, something out of this world.

E.T. Carbonell, Milt's
maternal grandfather, at the
turn of the century: "He had
an inappropriate love of
justice; never too much good
for his reputation."

Milt's mother Helen
in the 1920s, before
she got married.

Milt's father Robert, leading his reserve troops.

Milt as a healthy baby, before ill-health set in.

Milt at the age of twelve, always looking for his next fight.

Milt with his Grandmother Carbonell and two neighbours, in 1931.

Milt's mother, and his sisters Helen and Mary, in the mid-1950s.

Milt (second from left) looking dapper at his brother Robert's wedding.

Milt and Gwendolyn MacEwen on their wedding day in 1962:
"Just a couple of nuts."

Milt in Charlottetown at a family picnic in the summer of 1954.

Milt with Gwen at a party at Raymond Souster's house, circa 1960.

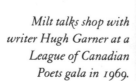

Milt talks shop with writer Hugh Garner at a League of Canadian Poets gala in 1969.

A police officer writes Milt a ticket for public speaking in Toronto's Allan Gardens as Joe Rosenblatt looks on, 1962. (Harry McLorinan/The Globe & Mail)

The Acorn clan gathers at mother Helen's 75th birthday party.

Poet Eli Mandel presents Milt with the People's Poet Award at Grossman's Tavern in Toronto in 1970. (J. Lewcun/The Globe & Mail)

Milt receives an honourary doctorate from the University of Prince Edward Island in 1977.

A haunting portrait of Milt and Gwen. (Michel Lambeth/Art Gallery of Ontario)

The last known photo of Milt, taken in his apartment in Charlottetown in 1986.

Natural Selection

> In the elephant's five-pound brain
> Poems are composed as a silent substitute for laughter....
> —"The Natural History of Elephants," from
> *I've Tasted My Blood*

VERY LITTLE OF MILTON ACORN'S WORK REMAINS IN PRINT. Fortunately, McClelland & Stewart recently reprinted *Dig Up My Heart*, his selected poems, which is readily available. The following "natural selection" offers some pertinent Acorn poems that didn't make it into the body of the text. For the CD-literate, consider this section Milt's "boxed set," containing his greatest hits, and alternative takes and rare cuts previously available only to collectors. The poems are arranged chronologically, which allows readers not only to trace Milt's development as a writer, but to follow the development of Canadian poetry as well. Some poems discussed in the text are not included here, notably "Homage To El Cortijo" and "On Shaving Off His Beard" (the source for the title of this book). Neither of these poems are complete, although James Deahl is currently piecing together an authoritative version of "On Shaving Off His Beard." Any other anomalies will be explained along the way. Starting with *I've Tasted My Blood*, Milt essentially put his poems in the public domain. He sincerely believed that poetry had the power to improve the human condition, and like other necessities of life—medical care, food, housing—they should be freely available for anyone who needed them.

Bibliography

In Love and Anger (self-published, 1956)

Against a League of Liars (Hawkshead Press, 1960)

The Brain's the Target (Ryerson Press, 1960)

Jawbreakers (Contact Press, 1963)

I've Tasted My Blood: Poems 1956 to 1968 (Ryerson Press, 1969)

More Poems for People (NC Press, 1972)*

The Island Means Minago (NC Press, 1975)*

Jackpine Sonnets (Steel Rail, 1977)*

Captain Neal MacDougal & the Naked Goddess (Ragweed Press, 1982)

Dig Up My Heart: Selected Poems, 1952-1983 (McClelland & Stewart, 1983)*

Whiskey Jack (HMS Press, distributed by Mekler & Deahl, Publishers, 1986)*†

A Stand of Jackpine (with James Deahl) (Unfinished Monument Press, 1987)*†

The Uncollected Acorn (edited by James Deahl) (Deneau Publishers, 1987)†

I Shout Love and Other Poems (edited by James Deahl) (Aya Press, 1987)*†

Hundred Proof Earth (edited by James Deahl) (Aya Press, 1988)*†

To Hear the Faint Bells (Unfinished Monument Press, distributed by Mekler & Deahl, Publishers, 1996)*†

*In print at press time.

†Published posthumously.

NOTE: I Shout Love and Other Poems and *Hundred Proof Earth* were published by Aya Press, which changed its name to The Mercury Press. *Whiskey Jack* and *To Hear the Faint Bells* are both available from Mekler & Deahl, Publishers, c/o 237 Prospect Street South, Hamilton, Ontario, L8M 2Z6.

Filmography

In Love and Anger: Milton Acorn, Poet (National Film Board, 1984)
A Wake For Milton (National Film Board, 1988)

Recordings

Milton Acorn reading from More Poems for People (SpareTime Editions, Box 596, Station A, Fredericton, NB E3B 5A6)

The National Milton Acorn Festival

For information on Prince Edward Island's annual Milton Acorn Festival, contact 902-894-8766.

A Chill Poem

If I, on a lonely road,
Meet a demon in the night,
His wild eyes gleaming hungrily,
All quivering with an urge insane,
Stemming from ardor I cannot fight
To quench a thirst I cannot ken;

Then I will know the spiny thrill
That chills a night-bound jungle beast
When he scents a great cat on his trail.

1945, unpublished. Acorn's earliest surviving poem. It's decidedly
"modern," and in ways superior to many poems that followed. Al-
though he dated the poem 1945, it seems too "clean," and I suspect this
is a revised version of the original, now lost.

Grey Girl's Gallop

(The scene: a country fair)

A merry-go-round hangs music on the air
That bubbles like a live electric brook.
It's all unseen
This is the track
With all the midway's joys behind the back
Of filling stands, serene, white-washed and worn.
And on the track, intent upon their business,
Stern drivers put the racers through their paces;
All rapt, intense, their whole selves concentrated,
Immersed within the bodies of their charges;
Feeling as they feel, with dedicated difference,
For this man-horse communion spans the distance
From primal urge to mankind's lofty purpose.
The very gait that's ordered's an invention;
A smoothened thing, man-designed, which exchanges
Speed for the essence of speed, and changes
The awkward onrush for the streamlined effort;
Straining the beasts to things of fire and wonder.
And now; a lull—The track is clear.
Then, through the gateway with a lunge and veer
Comes a grey-coated, bucking, wilful mare,
Who tries immediately to break and run.
Her driver grits his teeth and pulls the reins
And Grey Girl, though she fights and strains,
Is settled to a precise soldier-trot.

(The play begins)

"Oh for a gallop, one good gallop!
Just let me hit the ground with a wallop!

Just to release my inhibitions!
To hell with trotting and its traditions!"
Thus thought Grey Girl on that golden midday
With a fresh breeze blowing and noise from the midway,
"Oh for a gallop!"

They'll tell you a mare has no opinions:
Reflexes, working like gears and pinions,
Thoughtlessly sort out her stark impressions
Robotly come up with her expressions.
Well—Man is the same, at least some consider.
It's not sense that pulls him hither and thither
But only the play of his wilful emotions
Which he dresses up with fanciful notions.
Raging, he holds his body assizes;
Then to explain the whole thing he rationalizes!
That may be the truth but it's due to his nurture:
He's born for a god, for a molder of nature.
And further—the truth of the matter is shocking—
Those are to blame who do the most mocking.
So let us pretend that the mare reasons thoughtfully,
'Cause though there's a difference there might as well not be!
Consider Grey Girl who's been chafing all morning,
Now fighting the bit with its tugging warning,
On fire for a gallop.

The sun and the wind together are bracing;
With the track not too dry it's a good day for racing.
The stands are alive and eager and humming.
Bright-eyed and excited the crowd keeps coming,
From out of the town with its sun-baked pavements
Or from the red plowland's back-breaking enslavements;
From whatever to them is familiar, prosaic,
To this which is glamorous, wild and heroic.
They come for the joy, the color, the clamor,
But once they're inside they're assailed with this yammer:

"Quick—Get down your bets!" The tone is stentorian
From a righteous loud-speaker, so authoritarian
That greed seems the thing, and a lot of them scurry
As told to, to get down their bets in a hurry;
Each hoping to gain at the expense of the others:
Only thus do the rich make the workers their brothers.
Who heard of a tempter who used his dupe squarely!
From each bet put down there's subtracted unfairly
Twenty percent of the dough of the winner
For five minutes work! Whose roll won't be thinner
At the end of a day of that kind of dealing?
Some call it business but I call it stealing!
Enough of those robbers—the crowd is expectant
though soon a good half will be broke and repentant.
They consider Grey Girl and their chances of making
Some money on her, but don't guess how she's aching
Like mad for a gallop.

Now, Grey Girl's a female who's heedless and wily;
When she can't get her way she begins to get guiley.
If her driver is set on this disciplined goose-step
He'd better watch out or she'll give him an upset.
He's rounding a turn and his left wheel is grazing.
He sees that one moment; next moment he's gazing
Up into the clouds with a stupid expression
Flat on his back, and his mind forms a question:
What is that noise for? The answer is stunning:
The crowd has gone wild 'cause Grey Girl is running
All by herself with nobody to mind her,
Mane flying and sulky bouncing behind her;
Off on her gallop.

"Oh joy what a gallop! What a wonderful gallop!
Lovely to hit the ground with a wallop;
Flying, feeling my muscles contracting,
Shaking the soil with a fearful impacting,

Then hurtling on in delirious bounces,
Whole body exploding in power-surging jounces;
Not the prim pretty gait of civilization
But a passionate rout—pure barbarization!
What a glorious gallop!"

While with pure joy Grey Girl was gone hazy
Everyone else on those grounds had gone crazy.
They couldn't know her exalted condition
Now that she'd ripped off her pants of 'hibition.
Some yelled for fear disaster would find her
Through the broken sulky bouncing behind her;
And there were those who found it comical,
Who urged her on with cheers ironical.
She tore past the stands with her mane and tail flowing,
A wild white vision—and such shouting and "whoaing!"
Set up—begun by just one idiot—
If she'd wanted to panic she'd certainly had it.
But her soul had taken wings and remembered,
Before her people were tamed and encumbered,
When they played on the steppes with their wild hooves flying;
Racing and mating, fighting and dying.
Instead of the track-dust her hard hooves were crushing
The gay-colored steppe-flowers; her nostrils were rushing
Through clean-scented steppe-air, as wild as her nature
Before it had tasted the obstinate nurture
Of neck-hurting check-rein, of gait-forcing halters,
And all of the paraphernalia that alters,
Imposes the pattern of standardization
To the tight requirements of civilization:
Won't let a girl gallop.

By the track was a dog who was getting suspicious
This mare was opposing the master's wishes.
When she passes he's sure, and a white fluff of fury
Tears out, a righteous one-canine jury,

Barking his rage at this evil-doer,
Hurtling with dutiful zeal to pursue her.
With a rocketing spurt he overtakes her,
And with small-dog wrath he berates her;
For a moment partakes of the master's importance,
Then he's winded and left behind in abortence.
But he's not down-hearted; he's tasted the savor
Of glory—of doing the Great Ones a favour.
He dog-trots off with his tail standing proudly,
With his head held high though he's panting loudly.
Sad to say no-one sees him; they're all yelling and glaring
Across to the back-stretch where Grey Girl is tearing
On her mad gallop.

The next time around it's a like-to-be hero,
Initiative high, intelligence zero,
Who vaults the stretch-fence with athletic perfection.
"Stay away from that horse!" a bull-throated direction
Roars from the loud-speaker, for a while previous voiceless
With his pride injured now the poor fool is choiceless.
He leaps out in front of her, prancing and waving
For a moment, then he has to jump and's left raving;
Obscening to cover his sore of humility
While the heartless crowd mocks at his futility;
While again round the turn in her mad career,
Having now left a fast-traveled mile to the rear,
Still Grey Girl galloped.

Up in the stands there was one who'd watched coldly,
Now runs her name through with a lead-pencil boldly.
His lips curl down hard on his frustrated anger
Not mildly (for this was a curse) he says, "Dang her!"
He is a horse-player who'd trembled and pondered
Till he'd made his mind up to put money on her.
"The devil! She's running herself to a frazzle!"
The clamor, the joy, the keenness and dazzle

Are lost on this man, absorbed in the futile
Battle of odds with the pari-mutuel.
"She coulda' fixed me—She coulda' did it!
This is what happens each time that I hit it!"
And while like a fool he tore up his tickets
What passed for his mind dreamed up punishments wicked
For her and her gallop!

Now the Girl's had her gallop, her hot breath is soughing,
While through her great arteries a hard pulse is rowing;
Her spirited leaps are now efforted jumping;
The beat of her hooves is a gut-shaking thumping.
She's not quite exhausted; it's just that she's sated;
The tormenting clutch at her nerves has abated:
For they each had been pulled to piano-wire tightness,
Till she'd taken to galloping's primitive rightness.
She's ready to stop now, if someone will catch her;
And she veers without heart from the next bridle-snatcher.
Quiescent, she's pulled to a stop by the stables
By a lad who had watched till he thought he was able
To do it—The audience roars with approval;
But the unimpressed speaker booms out for removal.
"Unharness her first—That sulky is broken."
It's almost an insult; he needn't have spoken.
This boy knows his business, he's moving already,
While his voice reassures her with tone soft and steady.
At that he's misjudged her, she'd never been frightened;
She feels that a terrible burden has lightened:
On account of her gallop.

"Just wait," thinks Grey Girl, "till I'm rested:
that track-record's gonna be bested.
Just watch me now that I've had my fun;
I'll show 'em how trotting oughta be done!"
Nobody knows what goes on in her head,
They're scratching her off of their cards instead.

Only her owner looks at her eyes,
Stands pursing his lips and seeming wise:
"I don't think that break has done 'er;
Go tell the judges I'm gonna run 'er.
No wait —" he's figured an angle that's neat,
"Tell 'em we wanta skip the first heat:
She's tired from her gallop!"

In ending this yarn I confess to confusion:
The thing has concluded before its conclusion.
Oh—the Girl won two heats to the joy of short-enders;
The fool eased his pride in a dilly of benders;
The dog lived his days with a fond recollection
Of how he'd stood up to a monstrous defection:
Each kick in his ribs seemed thus compensated.
And if you're inclined to feel sympathetic
Towards the horse-player—don't—the synthetic
World that he lived in hung less upon earnings
Than on his justification. The spurnings
Of him by the fates inflated his ego;
For since he was markedly luckless then, ergo,
The world was conferring on him the distinction
Of arranging affairs to effect his extinction!
A silly idea, I'll grant, but it saved him
From feeling a cog in the grind that enslaved him.
So do the effects of one phase of the system
Turn into more profits—
              I'll just be old-fashioned
And end with a moral. You will note the impassioned
Gallop of Grey Girl had no special purpose
But only to do it and use up her surplus
Of joy, which once spurned cannot be collected.
As for those who did things because they expected
To harvest a profit of money or glory—
Well, whether they managed it isn't the story:
But Grey Girl was sure from the moment she started

To get what she asked for. When life was imparted
To men and to horses both races knew this
"A thing is well done which is done for its own bliss
Or else done for life—living now or begotten."
Most horses remember:
        Most men have forgotten.

Winter 1953, *New Frontiers*. Acorn's literary career began with this poem, published in Margaret Fairley's left wing magazine *New Frontiers*. He was almost thirty when it was published, and while it's a competent piece of work, with flashes of intelligence and humour, it's not the kind of poem I'd expect from a young poet in tune with the times. Despite its political content, the poem's style is closer to the Romantic tradition than to modernism (which was already old hat in 1953, and giving way to postmodernism). The narrative structure, which Acorn called "trail-blazing," is nothing new. Also, here we see how he frequently sacrificed good sense to the gods of rhyme (anger/"Dang her!"; clamour/yammer). None of this is a criticism of him. Acorn always said that politics was his first love, and that he came to poetry rather late in life.

Norman Bethune, died Nov. 13, 1939

We carried him who'd often carried us—
Spiritually, by purpose, and by scorn
Which rooted in his love could just be borne
—all through the suffering night and, in a house
(One of a village ugly as a louse—
Except its people) let him rest. The morn
Broke greyly as he woke. Great sobs were torn
From us to note his worn-out gentleness.

Then, like a bruised and helpless child, I prayed,
Not knowing whether to a god or him,
To curse and drag himself up by life's rim,
Angelic fire and pity to our aid.
But he, it seemed the moment he replied:
"No Tung—You live—And make improvements!" died.

———————

Fall 1953, *New Frontiers*. Acorn was already improving. This fourteen-line sonnet about the greatest hero of the Canadian left is a much more sophisticated poem than "Grey Girl's Gallop." There's still the awkward rhyme (house/louse), but his command of tone and emotion has started to surface. This poem is an example of the McGill Movement's brand of modernism: the language reflects everyday speech, the subject matter is an ordinary, although heroic, man. Acorn quickly mastered the sonnet form, which perfectly suited his rhetorical tendencies, and turned to it again and again throughout his life.

The Slum House

Who will buy a slum house?
Just look at that sign!
"For Sale," it says, on a leaky dump
That isn't fit for swine.

Who will buy a slum house?
What kind of fool will buy
A place where it's hard to stay alive
And harder still to die?

Can you buy a slum house?
You got the money? Yeah,
Coughs and chills and, best of all,
Virus pneumonia!

You won't live there—Oh dear no!
Just sit back and trust
God will send you lots of folks
Who'll live there 'cause they must.

For every creaky floorboard
You'll get a dollar bill,
One from every rat-hole, ten
For a rotten window sill!

There's even a street-car goes past.
Ain't it got a craw!
You jam cattle in like that
And you'll hear from the law!

Wait'll I tell my baby's kids.
Won't they be surprised

When I say even misery
Was once commercialized!

1954, *The Uncollected Acorn*. During the 1940s, the McGill Movement, which was a general rejection of the Romantic in favour of the modern, gave way to social realism, a kind of modern poetry that emphasized the plight of the common man ("plight" being the operative word). "The Slum House" is an example of this social realist style, and also shows how strongly Acorn's writing was influenced by "oral" poets like Joe Wallace. It's easy to imagine him standing up at a union hall or a meeting of the Labour Progressive Party and reciting this poem to cheers and approving applause. In fact, this was what the social realist movement was trying to do: revitalize poetry and make it relevant to the lives of everyday people. Having the advantage of not coming from an academic or literary background, Acorn quickly mastered this style of writing and made it his own.

Of Martyrs

> I often think of martyrs
and when I do the cosmos shakes
and with that pity I can touch their time
>> can feel their flesh
>>> for they were the most loving of folk.

> It was life they chose
not death
not the myriad little deaths that leave life a shadow
>> a ghost
>>> a memory un-remembered.

> How strong they were!
How vibrant was their walk,
heedful of deepest right, entirely living,
>> up to the door of death
>>> which they swung wide!

> Singers they were
who would not lop one verse
from the song of their lives, who would not say
>> the dull fantastic prose
>>> the crazy chants of liars.

> And the door of their deaths is an open door
into the paradise of life
where the song of their lives goes on, where it leaps
>> to our own vocal chords
>>> and sets them singing.

> It is the garden of life
the home of all us living

who choose not death but life . . . choose the clear eyes
    the bold voice
       and the mind like lightening.

Winter 1955, *New Frontiers*. "Of Martyrs" is a stunning achievement, the first real indication that Milton Acorn was a poet to be reckoned with. He abandoned the trappings of Romanticism (although he remained a Romantic at heart), and in the process, found a powerful poetic voice. I suspect, by the way, that it was written with Ethel and Julius Rosenberg in mind. Acorn constantly revised his poems; readers can find a very different version of "Of Martyrs" in *Dig Up My Heart*.

To My Little Sister About Her Illness

My little sister, you were the youngest.
'Til you were ten we used to call you "Baby,"
but then our mother put a stop to it
for fear they'd name you "Babe."

Yet you were always determined
to sip life's sweetest, most ephemeral juices . . .
To sip them lightly, and with no abandon:
so until now you've lived
like a silver water-bug
skating over the sun-blue lake of your youth.

Know then, my little sister:
that where black seas crash against riven rock
their roaring drowns out neither life nor thought;
that in the stronghold of endurance
the coins of life are counted one-by-one;
and sometimes in the pauses of the storm,
when the sun strikes many-colored on the battlements
of new clouds rolling westward on their thunders
a glory can strike you
greater than a lightning bolt.

———————

1956, *In Love and Anger*. The stand-out from Acorn's first (and self-published) book, and his first exceptional poem. Here he is continuing the work he started in "Of Martyrs," exploring that mystical vision that was the source of his best work and which lifts the poet to a level that transcends labels like Romanticism and modernism. Its form is unusual, a kind of extended sonnet that Acorn would much later christen "jackpine sonnet." It was written for his youngest sister, Helen, who would die of cancer only a few months before he passed away.

Lyric

If I said love that word
'd recreate me as love;
said love you that breathe
'd drop me trembly on
your breasts, your breath.

Love's before you, before me;
nearest to god we know.
Utter his name truly then he
's possessor and law.
Listen, love, I say it.

———————

1958, *Yes*. Acorn's first purely literary poem, showing that he was quickly mastering his craft. "Lyric" expands on the formal experiments begun with "Of Martyrs." (Note: the last word in the third line is "breathe" in the original; it may correctly be "breath".)

I've Tasted My Blood

If this brain's over-tempered
consider that the fire was want
and the hammers were fists.
I've tasted my blood too much
to love what I was born to.

But my mother's look
was a field of brown oats, soft-bearded;
her voice rain and air rich with lilacs:
and I loved her too much to like
how she dragged her days like a sled over gravel.

Playmates? I remember where their skulls roll!
One died hungry, gnawing grey porch-planks.
One fell, and landed so hard he splashed.
And many and many
come up atom by atom
in the worm-casts of Europe.

My deep prayer a curse.
My deep prayer the promise that this won't be.
My deep prayer my cunning,
my love, my anger,
and often even my forgiveness,
that this won't be and be.
I've tasted my blood too much
to abide what I was born to.

April 1958, *Delta*. If anyone had doubts about Acorn's skills, this poem set
them to rest. "I've Tasted My Blood" was a completely original expression of
intelligence and passion; no one had ever written a poem quite like it.

I Shout Love

I shout love in a blizzard's
scarf of curling cold,
for my heart's a furred sharp-toothed thing
that rushes out whimpering
when pain cries the sign writ on it.

I shout love into your pain
when skies crack and fall
like slivers of mirrors,
and rounded fingers, blued as a great rake,
pluck the balled yarn of your brain.

I shout love at petals peeled open
by stern nurse fusion-bomb sun,
terribly like an adhesive bandage,
for love and pain, love and pain,
are companions in this age.

1958, *I Shout Love and Other Poems*. This is the original version of the famous "I Shout Love," and in this short form, it's as powerful a poem as "I've Tasted My Blood." This poem is fueled by Acorn's love of the dialectic, the official philosophy of the Communist International, which he loosely interpreted as the "contradictions of everyday life." While dialectics informed much of his poetry, and guided his interpretation of the world, this poem was Acorn's finest expression of this philosophy.

Charlottetown Harbor

An old docker with gutted cheeks,
time arrested in the used-up-knuckled hands
crossed on his lap, sits
in a spell of the glinting water.

He dreams of times in the cider sunlight
when masts stood up like stubble;
but now a gull cries, lights,
flounces its wings ornately, folds them,
and the waves slop among the weed-grown piles.

––––––––––

Fall 1958, *The Fiddlehead*. Perhaps Acorn's best-known poem—a simple, brilliantly descriptive lyric. Its earliest appearance is in a letter to his mother a few months before publication, under the title "Charlottetown Water."

Pastoral

That sudden time I heard
the pulse of song in a thrush throat
my windy vision fluttered
like snow-clouds buffeting the moon.

Soldier's son and soldier, born to
rubbish and monotony raked by death;
depression child, lucky but
cut by the looks of thin kin faces:

yet that song, and the drop-notes
of a brook truckling thru log-brakes and cedar,
I came to on numb, clumsy limbs,
to find outside the beauty inside me.

1958, unpublished. This is the original version of an oft-collected poem
(first published in *The Fiddlehead*, Fall 1959), taken from a letter to his
mother. By now, Acorn was one of the more promising of the new
breed of Montreal poets, which also included his friend Al Purdy. The
poem is a significant expression of his commitment to the modernist
movement. A pastoral was a favourite Romantic form, an extended
rumination on nature and the beauty of natural design. In Acorn's
modern pastoral, the poet must retreat within himself to rediscover
"the beauty" that humanity has banished from the outside world.

Problem

When you look into your golden beer
and talk about suicide, Al,
I can't help dreaming laments,
obituaries, and how craftily
I'd cull my quotations
of you; half martyr
to this dusty tasting time
and half damned decadent.

Like a green lignum vitae tree,
a nuisance on the lawn,
dead you'd carve into strong shapes,
living you're a problem.

––––––––––––

1959, *Moment #1*. Milton Acorn had a wonderful sense of humour, although it rarely made its way into his poems. In the fourth edition of *I've Tasted My Blood*, he explains that "the lignum vitae tree will grow in almost any pollution, hence its name 'vitae'—'living'. It is also lethal—poisoning the grass around its trunk."

The Fights

What an elusive target
the brain is! Set up
like a coconut on a flexible stem
it has 101 evasions.
A twisted nod slews a punch
a thin gillette's width
past a brain, or
a rude brush-cut to the chin
tucks one brain safe under another.
Two of these targets are
set up to be knocked down
for twenty-five dollars or a million.

In that TV picture in the parlour
the men, though linked move to move
in the chancy dance,
are abstractions only.
Come to ringside, with two
experts in there! See
each step or blow pivoted,
balanced and sudden as gunfire.
See muscles wriggle, shine
in sweat like windshield rain.

In stinking dancehalls, in
the forums of small towns,
punches are cheaper but
still pieces of death.
For the brain's the target
with its hungers
and code of honour. See
in those stinking little towns,

with long counts, swindling judges,
how fury ends with the last gong.
No matter who's the cheated one
they hug like a girl and man.

It's craft and
the body rhythmic and terrible,
the game of struggle.
We need something of its nature
but not this;
for the brain's the target
and round by round it's whittled
till nothing's left of a man
but a jerky bum, humming
with a gentleness less than human.

October 1960, *The Canadian Forum*. Acorn had by now completely
abandoned pentameter, and, despite his interest in the McGill Move-
ment, was slipping into a style that appeared to be almost experimen-
tal. He would, however, never abandon his political and rhetorical
stances—which on the one hand align him with a populist, oral tradi-
tion in Canada, and on the other, set him at odds with the pure poetry
of the *Tish* group. In any case it's one of Acorn's finest poems. As a kid,
he dreamed of becoming a professional boxer; instead, he took on the
entire world. The last line is particularly poignant, in light of his final
days.

Letter to My Redheaded Son

Young maple leaves, copper with delicate flush,
are taut and hardly bent by the limb-twist breeze,
and I'm penetrated by the delight that made you
and makes fool poets call the spring green.

A poet against a league of liars, I know
you'll learn love and honesty from her
who wouldn't learn scorn and left me.
You'll learn, boy, to be as bitter as me
against the men with counterfeit eyes,
their graft and their words: "nigger,"
"people not like us" . . . and "bastard."

Fool poets call the spring green, but I
a poet, know I can't give you to yourself
—only what I know of myself: that
nothing I've done, no poem, stand,
thought or act of love, hasn't called for
another, stronger deed, or I've lost it.

1960, *Against a League of Liars*. The best piece from the broadside published by John Robert Colombo. The poem was written for Milt's son, born around 1956. Milt did not marry the boy's mother, and the son was put up for adoption. This incident troubled him, and he spent much of his final years trying to track his son down. Once again, the form is interesting, an early example of the loosely structured "jackpine sonnet."

Pit Accident

"I liked him," said the small man
with coal seaming his hard little hands,
"because he never stood in your light."

"It must've been a bad twinge,
in the bone, not the muscle,
that made him shift and lift his head,
riding down to work, and
that beam came up too quick to blink at."

"He never stood in your light, poor guy."
He was pale, though as a root at bedrock,
but tears squeezed out on his rigid face
and even the rain tasted of coaldust.

1960, *Against a League of Liars*. An early example of the kind of short
narrative poem that Acorn perfected (and a great improvement on the
ponderous "Grey Girl's Gallop"). He claimed that all his narrative
poems were based on true life experiences. I don't think he ever
worked in a mine—although it's conceivable that he did do some
carpentry for one.

I Shout Love

I shout Love in a land muttering slack damnation
as I would in a blizzard's blow,
staggering stung by snowfire in the numbing tongues of cold,
for my heart's a furry sharp-toothed thing
that charges out whimpering
even when the pain cries the sign written on it.

I shout Love even tho it might deafen you
and never say that Love's a mild thing
for it's hard, a violation
of all laws for the shrinking of a people.
I *shout* Love, counting on the hope
that you'll sing and not shatter in Love's vibration.

I shout Love . . . Love . . . It's a net
scooping us weltering, fighting for joy
hearts beating out new tempos against each other.

The wild centre of life explodes from a seed
recreates me daily in your eyes' innocence
as a small ancient creature, Love's inventor,
listened to a rainbow of whispers.

I shout Love against the proverbs of the damned
which then pause between clubbings and treacheries
to quote with wise communicative nods . . . I know
they're lies, but know too
that if I declared a truce in this war
they'd turn into pronged truths and disembowel me.

By what grim structure in the skull
do you justify unloveliness? I tell you

this machine has masters
who play their contradiction of music on you.

I shout Love against my prison where unconscious joy
like a brown sparrow chirping hoppity zig-zag
seems my keeper ... In his bright ignorant eye
I live a prisoner while masons plonk stone
to soak up sunlight meant for prisoners
each one a piece of my brain, fragment of my heart's muscle.

And prisoners with hunger aching like a tooth in the belly;
          All the robbed ones—
wonderless kids,
              strengthless men,
                        women with no vision for their womb-thoughts.
How'll I escape? Clang shut my own cell door?

I shout Love for all the colors and shapes of men,
all their subtleties
of blood and bone, thought and vision:
imagining for each
a destiny according to his particular beauty.

I shout Love for the womanflower, the manflower,
and don't too carefully tend them.
Inventing themselves moment by moment
out of joy, sorrow
and stark machinery of need
what do they need of me before my truth?

I shout Love ... which is just the beginning:
Truth ... which is just the beginning:
Honor ... which is just the beginning:
And sometimes turn from the long-fanged enemy
To eat the worm in my own heart.

Louis Riel, that man sad with wisdom
I Love . . . and his hope Canada:
for hopes are the taller parts of men,
my stilts and eyes' loving perspective,
hope my liver pumping the bile that is life.

Does any one know where the corpse is buried?
Under whose stuffed seat? What dancer's foot?
Louis Riel I Love
but the hangman drives to a Sunday picnic with his family
and whatever the martyr gained he claims.

I shout Love for this Earth all corseted and raked by Man.
Unloving the deeds done on her
but I mean Love.

Even I shout Love who aged ten thousand years
before my tenth birthday
in shame, wrath, and wickedness;
shout and grow young as cowards grow old:
Shout Love whom this world's paradoxical joy
makes stammer or keep silent between shoutings,
more held each hour by the wonder of it.

I shout You my Love in a springtime instant
when I wince half pain half joy to notes from an oriole
over balls of frost trapped in quickening roots,
and the tick-tock-tickle of warm rain
trickling into buds' eyes, plucking them open.

I shout Love into your pain when times change and you must change:
minutes seeming final as a judge's sentence
when skies crack and fall
like splinters of mirrors
and gauntlette fingers, blued as a great rake,
pluck the balled yarn of your brain:

For Love's the spine holding me straight,
the eye in back of my shoulderblades
that sees and beats my heart for all thinkers,
and the touch all over and thru me
I've often called God.

The herring with his sperm make milk of the wide wrinkling
   wriggling ocean
where snowy whales jump rolling among whitecaps
as I shout Love your Love and the deeds of my words
pollinate the air you're breathing.
Since life's a dream garment hung singing or sighing on a bone tree
why shouldn't it be Love's adventure?

I shout Love between your knees that are my wings my Love,
when I ride like a dragon
blessing your fierce as curses.
Oh take me Love for I'm a storm of light
enwhorled with satanic darkness.

I whisper Love into the ear of a newborn girl,
breathing Love in her name.
May she grow up around her name singing inside her.
I shout Love against Death, that rattling, stinking harvest machine
the loves best the ripest and richest in Love.
I've seen their eyes bright with hunger
gorging on their last light;
and felt Love lurch sidling away
from the small help they wanted.

I shout Love and am no sentimentalist
for I rejoice in the deaths of rogues.

But Love like thrilling roots
like nerves digging the buried corpse,

the old fierce eye rotted and born new,
an enemy lost in a lover.

I shout Love wherever there's loveless silence;
in dumb rocks, in black iron lie oppressed minds
like parsecs of night between the stars,
where suns in tumultuous sleep toss eruptions about them
and I wake with a cry
spinning among the galaxies.

I shout Love to the young whose eyes are clouded with light
as their light clouds my eyes.
Only as beards of wheat swaying at the fingertips may I touch them
for they're born in the centre, are the centre,
and I shout Love, even tho
they're something of me they must destroy.

You to whom honor came so easily
in your darling girl world,
when your joy changed so quickly to defiance
you shocked us but
you made our hearts and brains beat one rhythm
and we followed you.

I shout Love at those grey-lipped men who trim life:
Shout Love into their dim tears, their shaking heads.

I shout Love to you, Flesh humming thoughts, blood's rhythm,
intricate bonework, hair played in by wind,
and your words jostling, seeking
things growing or still, peopled, mysteries, yourself
with your soles touching the grass for instants.

I Love the dawn, with a half-risen sun all rosy like the head of God's
  phallus.

But what if I came shouting Love now
to you shivering in your blanket
unfed for forty-eight hours?
The liberals goggle over their cocktails
to talk patiently of feeding you,
but I shout Love and I mean business.

I shout Love in those four-letter words
contrived to smudge and put it in a harmless place,
for Love today's a curse and defiance.
Listen you money-plated bastards
puffing to blow back the rolling Earth with your propaganda
       bellows and oh-so-reasoned negations of Creation:
When I shout Love I mean your destruction.

Spring 1963, *The Fiddlehead* (special issue). In 1961 Allen Ginsberg
wrote, "I have seen the best minds of my generation destroyed by
madness." Three years earlier, Milton Acorn first wrote, "I shout
love!" But it wasn't until 1963 that the poem reached its famous, epic
proportions. This is the version that prompted Fred Cogswell, *The
Fiddlehead*'s poetry editor, to devote an entire issue to Acorn's work. It
is also Joe Rosenblatt's favourite version: "Milt kept writing and re-
writing it," Rosenblatt complained. "He should have left it alone."
Along with "The Natural History of Elephants," this is Acorn's undis-
puted masterpiece.

The Damnation Machine

Hell's the place
of the disarmed innocents
who can't use the purge of rage.

It's long since they've been penetrated
by sorrow; their souls are
a smudged page
where nothing can be written.

All wars have been fought
and lost,
won,
or just gone by,
and the weapons of the mind
hang in a void.

(Meaningless chopped prose
without the rhythm of combat,
the painting done in blood
and blackness,
the sting of joy.)

Side by side the damned walk
heel and toe in old tracks.
Their words have no bearing
on questions they've almost forgotten.

———————

Spring 1963, *The Fiddlehead*. Acorn's finest "anti-war" poem, "The Damnation Machine" has been out of print for almost twenty years, and is now almost forgotten. When it was published, Acorn was at the height of his power as a "populist" poet who spoke in the everyday language of the common people. At the same time, his artistic gifts were unrivalled. He was unique: a poet who bridged Canada's oral and literary traditions.

Poem

My mother goes in slippers
and her weight thumps the floor,
but when I think of her I think of one smile
when she was young

and to me was a goddess of green age
tho now I remember her young
with hair red as a blossom.

I remember the whole room full of that smile
and myself scampering across the edges.

Now she lives on cigarettes and wine,
goes from potted plant to flower,
knowing the time and manner
of each one's tending.

———————

1963, *The Fiddlehead*. While Milt's father supplied the anger, his mother supplied the love. She doted on her eldest son his entire life. Helen Acorn objected to the last stanza, but Milt's brother Robert says while his mother didn't *live* on cigarettes and wine, she certainly enjoyed them.

Letter to Al Purdy

Dear Al:
One defends that tangle of roots
at the heart, the *me* first discovered
in childhood, colored so vividly then
and afterwards forgotten, until
some wound lets in the poison light.

A particle loose and battered
in a dying society, I've
reached the point where every human contact
brings pain: worst of all, any touch
of what's most human in me
. . . my poetry. Sheltered in a small room
of a mental hospital, I impale myself
when I can, on this bayonet.
Irving, Louis . . . each
has his cerebral bombshelter
as have many with a better excuse:
you and I are alike in that
we have none and want none.
I remember warning Joe
over a cup of coffee on Bloor Street:
"All right, be a poet, but
people are twisted—in pain
or curling inside themselves
to escape pain, and
once you get a conception of
what they ought to be . . .
Honesty's the first
and main tool

of a poet, and Joe
once you learn to look at people
honestly,
to look at yourself
honestly,
will you be able to stand it?"

---

c. 1963, unpublished. After his breakup with Gwendolyn MacEwen, Milt's emotional health deteriorated considerably. I found this undated poem in the archives and I believe he wrote it during his stay at the Westminster Veterans' Hospital in London. Besides Al Purdy, the other poets mentioned are Joe Rosenblatt, Irving Layton, and Louis Dudek.

Death Lyric

Death walks on padded feet
Soft as a pussycat, or a tiger,
And his face has chiseled shadows
Seen in the flare of a lighter.

Do you know the rapt silence
In the centre of a scream?
Where your days are measured
Light as a seed borne of the breath?

Or the infinitude of mirrors
That are his eyes? Faces
Of those you've tried to love,
Errors, and empty places

In what you've proudly called a soul?
Blessed are those who see a deed
That led fate two steps by the nose,
A curse scotched, a heart comforted.

Winter 1964, *The Fiddlehead*. Another example of the dark side that
emerged in Acorn's poems during the Vancouver years. Literary
magazines of the mid-sixties are full of uncollected and forgotten
Acorn poems. In one afternoon at the Victoria Public Li-
brary—which carries only a few little magazines—I found two
dozen Acorn poems that I'd never seen before. If some enterprising
graduate student did a thorough search, Canadian literature might
be greatly enriched; I am certain that there are more Acorn gems
waiting to be unearthed. A completely revised, and much inferior,
version, "Death Walks on Petty Feet," appears in *The Island Means
Minago*.

My Sight Sprang

My sight sprang open at
that flying mane of sunrise
colors mixed with a tarry roil
in the cauldron of worlds;
creation's acid-splatter growing
beauty's flower-tree and
mindless cannibals, cads,
rogues, godlings
talking bell-and-birdtones or noises
like some ugly-mouthed machine,
all decked out in figures of men.

It was growth sucking brains
as brain sucked growth,
sucked men . . . a myriad
brains with invisible growth
hurting to be visible, and
all tangled
exchanging torment and joy.

I saw creation taken charge of:
cauldrons, hammer-rung, suns
sucked like oranges, stars
picked like cherries, the
galaxy spun in novel colors,
jewelers gone wondrous mad
tinkering atoms; and
everywhere gesticulation, sweepers
wrestling for brooms, furious
enlargements, condemnations, trimmings . . .

And why? Isn't anything growing
a cosmos? Why be visible
if the bright eye looks inward?
But this they needed to learn glory,
were tailors
sewing comets, nebulae
into the robes of lighted souls.

Fall 1964, *The Fiddlehead*. A lost treasure from Acorn's Vancouver years, this comes from the same mystical place as works like "Sky's Poem For Christmas."

The War In Viet Nam

The star above my head
's a baby burning, hopelessly
beyond my blessing. If I kissed him
we'd both scream,

but at least the flame
'd touch us both
... one reality perceived
. As it stands

only he knows he exists
by pain's present virtue, and all
I can do is acknowledge the

vanishment of light he radiates
(my brainpan's transparent to it
's needles ... and as for the strange animals
of my imagination, they're harried on
, made to disappear
if they want to lie still)

.

November 1965, *Blew Ointment*. The experiments with form continue. However, this poem owes as much to "Charlottetown Harbor" as it does to Charles Olson and his "Projective Verse." During his Vancouver days, Milton was an early and outspoken opponent of the Vietnam War.

The Natural History of Elephants

In the elephant's five-pound brain
The whole world's both table and shithouse
where he wanders seeking for viandes, exchanging great farts
For compliments. The rumble of his belly
Is like the contortions of a crumpling planetary system.
Long has he roved, his tongue longing to press the juices
From the ultimate berry, large as
But tenderer and sweeter than a watermelon;
And he leaves such signs in his wake that pygmies have fallen
And drowned in his great fragrant marshes of turds.

In the elephant's five-pound brain
The wind is diverted by the draughts of his breath,
Rivers are sweet gulps, and the ocean
after a certain distance is too deep for wading.
The earth is trivial, it has the shakes
and must be severely tested, else
It'll crumble into unsteppable clumps and scatter off
Leaving the great beast bellowing among the stars.

In the elephant's five-pound brain
dwarves have an incredible vicious sincerity,
A persistent will to undo things. The beast cannot grasp
The convolutions of destruction, always his mind
Turns to other things—the vastness of green
And the frangibility of forest. If only once he could descend
To trivialities he'd sweep the whole earth clean of his tormentors
In one sneeze so mighty as to be observed from Mars.

In the elephant's five-pound brain
Sun and moon are the pieces in a delightfully complex ballgame
That have to do with him . . . never does he doubt

The sky has opened and rain and thunder descend
For his special ministration. He dreams of mastadons
And mammoths and still his pride beats
Like the heart of the world, he knows he could reach
To the end of space if he stood still and imagined the effort.

In the elephant's five-pound brain
Poems are composed as a silent substitute for laughter,
His thoughts while resting in the shade
Are long and solemn as novels and he knows his companions
By names differing for each quality of morning.
Noon and evening are ruminated on and each overlaid
With the taste of night. He loves his horny perambulating hide
As other tribes love their houses, and remembers
He's left flakes of skin and his smell
As a sign and permanent stamp on wherever he has been.

In the elephant's five-pound brain
The entire Oxford dictionary'ld be too small
To contain all the concepts which after all are too weighty
Each individually ever to be mentioned;
Thus of course the beast has no language
Only an eternal pondering hesitation.

In the elephant's five-pound brain
The pliable trunk's a continuous diversion
That in his great innocence he never thinks of as perverse,
The pieces of the world are handled with such a thrilling
Tenderness that all his hours
Are consummated and exhausted with love.
Not slow to mate every female bull and baby
Is blessed with a gesture grandly gracious and felt lovely
Down to the sensitive great elephant toenails.

And when his more urgent pricking member
Stabs him on its horrifying season he becomes

A blundering mass of bewilderment . . . No thought
But twenty tons of lust he fishes madly for whales
And spiders to rape them. Sperm falls in great gouts
And the whole forest is sticky, colonies of ants
Are nourished for generations on dried elephant semen.

In the elephant's five-pound brain
Death is accorded no belief and old friends
Are continually expected, patience
Is longer than the lives of glaciers and the centuries
Are rattled like toy drums. A life is planned
Like a brush-stroke on the canvas of eternity,
And the beginning of a damnation is handled
With great thought as to its middle and its end.

1966, *Blew Ointment*. Another poem that defies formal labels, both a period piece (as the unofficial anthem of Canada's counterculture) and a timeless masterpiece. I'd read it ten times before someone pointed out to me that it was, in fact, Acorn's autobiography.

Where is Che Guevara?

These are miraculous days . . . Worms sing! The sound
       from their burrows is as lively as birds
but not so pleasant. And right now they are singing
"Where is Che Guevera?"

Che Guevera is beauty . . . The terrible and persistent
       beauty that's the end of those who can't stand it,
The end of worms.
They fear him and can't stop thinking of him.
The newspapers are speculating.
President Johnson, busy breaking a treaty
As his forebearers used to do on the Indians,
And now he does on the entire world
. . . arranging the murder of a Vietnamese girl
three weeks old; pauses just an instant in
the middle of
       handing out a souvenir pen
to think
       Where is Che Guevera?
"Who are the people who know?"
He can't tell . . . He's made too many enemies.

He has many agents but no friends,
Has had mistresses but no lovers;
And he who's often invoked God in support of ungodly lies
Wishes that God would exist for a moment
to answer one prayer . . . Tell him:
"Where is Che Guevera?"

I'll tell you where Che Guevera is . . .
He moves
He moves with the dead and unforgotten.

He moves with the lost Indians of the Pampas, hordes
     and hordes of them, tall on their horses.
He moves before their high lances, shining close-up like
     their burnished copper reins, invisible like those
     reins at a distance.
He moves.
He moves with Spartacus, up the Appian Way, blinking
     away the tears of memory and fixing two
     feelingly fierce eyes on Rome—Citadel of deceit,
     of the cannibals who devour men slowly . . . not
     their bodies but their entire lives.
And the time has come round . . . The time has come
     round for the end of it all
So more importantly he moves with the living.

Oh you manipulators, you planners of sour lives and
     cheated deaths, you puppet masters
Who play with dolls who ache and grieve for the things
     you do to them in your playing,
Or perhaps you don't grieve any more, having forgotten or
     never known what living is like:
Did you not just now shiver violently
As if a tall seemingly clumsy man in rubber boots clumped
     over your graves?
It is Che Guevera . . . He moves.
He moves precisely . . . He moves discretely.
He moves like the scalpel in the long boney hands of
     a great surgeon.
The cancer shall be cut out, and certainly the patient
     will survive.

Does he move as a little black dog, trotting everywhere,
     perhaps at the heels of an imperialist, sniffing
     them, holding in his guts the secret of how they
     shall be tripped?
No he moves by a more powerful magic than that.

He hates joyfully, he loves bitterly.
This is the fate of a man who is a man in this present age
And Che Guevera has not foresworn it.
There are others, millions of them, who also hate joyfully
        and love bitterly,
And they are his magic . . . They are his mystery.

Oh you putters and takers, you reckoners of dollars
        in the millions
each digit of which is a piece of work, a piece of a life,
        usually a swindled piece:
Does conscience bother you, or rather regret?
Do you think you have botched your lives?
And botched other peoples' lives even worse:
You students in Canadian Universities
Learning how to botch your lives
And botch other peoples' lives even worse:
Who are perhaps cynical, refusing to believe that a life
        can be anything but botched;
Or perhaps incapable even of understanding the concept
        of what is life,
Really a life . . . Not botched:
Do you wonder "Where is Che Guevera?"
And does the thought make you unsteady, and do you
        clutch for support to the nearest lie to you?
Not the truth . . . That would be too awfully thrilling
        and demanding.
I tell you there are men on Earth who usually tell
        the truth.
I know
Because I am one of them,
And I know I'm not unique.

And I have chosen who I will believe
And what I will believe.
I have chosen to believe in the ultimate . . . the loveliest

thing I can imagine;
I have chosen to believe in you, not as you are
But as you should be . . . I believe in your happiest wishes . . .

May 1967, *The Georgia Straight*. Acorn wrote this poem to be read out loud, and in part it can only be understood by taking into account the effect it would have had on its audience. Regardless, this and many more of his oral poems stand up very well in print.

Didache

A true poem
embraces
a man, doesn't
describe him.

The literal
always clumps
peg-legged, since
the mindseye
misses something.

Some thing of you
must be added
to warm the figure
and that (the
artist's moment
of truth) beat

in time with
sing, howl, go
with that man like
a counter-melody in
his dance of live blood.

So to every deed,
thought of love
add, and from
every curse
subtract
something of yourself
in allowance
for the unknown.

Winter 1964, *The Fiddlehead*. Acorn often wrote essays that tried to sum up his theory of poetry, usually with mixed results. He suffered from a "poet's logic," and what made sense to him seemed contradictory and downright confusing to others. This is perhaps his definitive statement on the poet's art.

The Tamarack Review

I pronounce a servantes against The Tamarack Review
Who's turned down my loveliest poems. But
Why should I condemn those people
Since they know and I know
That my beauty's a gun aimed at their ugly hearts?

The bread of hate, the cheese of disgust,
Are what I eat for breakfast: And in my morning walk
My footsteps beat out the time for a litany of curses.
Human beings are not of one species;
Genetically perhaps—but the definer of the human is the mind
And deeds. Most of us are good, or try to be:
But there are men viler than the fiends of Hell.

An editor of The Tamarack Review
Rises in life by spiral motion
Up the tunnel to Lucifer's bowels:
His nose plows rapturously through the reeking piles;
His tongue sticks out and every crumb of the million and fifty-seven
    varieties
Of Satanic *merde* he encounters, he licks up as a duty.

Teddy Bear told me "Don't send your good poems
to The Tamarack Review: Send tongue-in-cheek
Poems solemn about funny things, liberal about villainous things."
I don't guarantee absolutely I'll never sell out
(Who can? Tho I don't think I will) But for the sell-out prices which
    are offered to poets . . .
Christ, you bastards, this soul is an authentic one
And expensive. Of course, I sent them my best poems.

For a woman to get published in The Tamarack Review
If she has a good husband, she must leave him;

Write sad existential letters about how he was so goddamn noble
She couldn't stand it, whilst laying the dirtiest bastards in town;
Then send poems to The Tamarack Review
More explicit than a marriage manual but not so passionate.

Picture an editor of The Tamarack Review
Squashed by the heel of a genuine poet—
His arms and legs twitch with delayed signals from a dying nervous
     system;
His tongue wiggles pathetically, trying to tell one more lie;
He tries to fart back on beautiful things, piss forward into the eyes of
     the just . . .
He can't manage either. All things end.

----

c. 1967, uncollected. Acorn started this poem in the early sixties, and finished it in Vancouver in 1967. Notice the attack on Gwen in the second to last stanza: the lines are taken almost verbatim from a letter he'd sent to her at the time. Despite the graphic imagery, this is one of my favourite Acorn poems; rarely has the writer's frustration with the editor been summed up with such vicious eloquence. This original version was not published until after his death. A slightly different version was published in *The Tamarack Review* in 1971, under the title "The Canada Goose Review." A "servantes," by the way, is a kind of Spanish curse-poem.

Ode to the Timothy Eaton Memorial Church

You get up on that cross
This time Brother . . .
A carpenter, you say, gave up His life for you
And another carpenter knocked together
Two stout sticks . . .
      How charming were the Proletarians of Old Times!
I'm afraid us modern crew can't manage
That kind of mental weather;
If what you cross your hearts with crossed fingers
To say is true

      To save your souls?
How quaint! Take me for instance
      —I'd like to stand in for the Devil on his day off :
How I'd stoke!
      Or
          To take a better image
With what gusto I'd stand on the podium/And wield my baton
To direct the instruments manned by the fiends of Hell—
Moans! Screams! Choked prayers and sincere curses!
      What cacophony! ! !

Don't twitch!
      Here's your crown of thorns Sir!
Bravely bear the royal pricks! You know
You were right—

      That vision of a decent Man
      A Good God even
Bearing all sorts of pains for the sake of sinners,
Or to put it more bluntly—the rich;
Does give a certain satisfaction

I'd say a certain peace of the spirit
As long as a few amendments are made
Like, You, the guilty
Suffering instead of the innocent . . .
Much as you lust for a pure paschal lamb
Paschal snakes are much more satisfactory
To me . . .
                    That's right!
            Don't be shy!
Lick off that bloody sweat! ! !
In such circumstances the tongue's better than kleenex,
Like candy on an exasperating day:
And while you're tasting that Savour—My small mercy
            —ponder on what your lying legend of a
Voluntarily
Suffering Christ really means.

———————

1972, *More Poems For People*. Despite its punctuation, one of the best poems in this book. It's in the same unconventional form—poetry as pure rhetoric—as "Where Is Che Guevera?" which caught the spirit of the moment: *More Poems for People* sold 10,000 copies. The Eaton Memorial Church actually exists, by the way; it's located beside Toronto's Eaton Centre.

In The Sky

The hawk swoops down upon three crows
But the crows have seen him;
Suddenly they become nimble
Their erraticness an advantage.

To the hawk's life, they'll give no tribute of death.
                    They attack and
In half a minute it's over.
Knowing the slightest tremor of the wind
The hawk can climb faster.

Soon the crows have forgotten
Will tell no stories, sing no songs of triumph.
Neither does the hawk know humiliation;
Skimming, finding the updraughts
He distances himself further and further
Smaller and smaller in the heights.

Tho he must find a victim or die
Urgency's no use to him.
He's not equipped to think of it.

Fall 1971, *Blackfish* #2. Some commentators—James Deahl among them—believe that Acorn's stance as the "People's Poet" in the early seventies undermined his writing, and I think there is some truth in this. "In The Sky" is a prototype of the lyrical-narrative Acorn would come to dub the "jackpine sonnet," a simpler form which invigorated his later writing.

Incident from the Land Struggle (1767-1873)

"Well sirs, then we're agreed on the plan.
Black John here will fire on this Englishman
And miss (make sure of that, lad
The battle depends on this)
One quarter mile on, White John
Will miss too, but closer, and if that
Stinking piece of rent-collecting manure
Who dares call himself a gentleman
Keeps on, Red John will shoot his horse.
Old John here will then happen along
And lend him his horse—the red stallion.
Once he's on that beast, no more worries
Except to collect the remains, living or dead
And carry them back to Charlottetown
And, of course demand our expenses
Be very particularly
                angry
                        about that."

_____

1975, *The Island Means Minago*. A piece representative of the historical poems that dominates the new material in this collection. Although it won the Governor General's Award for Poetry, I think it's one of Acorn's weakest books. He always had a thing against theme books and *The Island Means Minago* proves that he should have trusted his initial impulses.

Rej at the Gears

No fish so weird, in salt-sweaty
Glass tank sea as you are
Manipulating your great harvester
With a happy quizzical
Look of power . . .

Sorcerer thinking new magic
While your machine raves songs
Like souls shaking chains;
You'll suck your own marrow
To spit stains on the sky
To give the day, tomorrow
A new bokay of tricks.

1976, *East of Canada: An Atlantic Anthology* (Breakwater Books). Mainstream critics believe that by the mid-seventies Milton had run out of gas. In fact, his powers remained intact, and the hits tended to outnumber the misses. As with the Vancouver work, a lot of this era's poems remain uncollected and forgotten. Note: "bokay" is Acorn's spelling.

Hope Begins Where False Hope Ends

Hope begins where false hope ends:
The strongest hope, made certain to win—
Tool redesigned, perfect in heft and fit.
If you sing in one key with the spheres
Ignoble in no aspect, the mending begins
Of all your losses, breakage, all those errors.
The strongest bone is one broken and mended.

The strongest brain has conceived a fool theory,
Researched, contrived, argued its defense
Then given up in face of evidence;
Or else stayed strong against a rally of prejudice
Because its truth keeps some part unwearied;
Until one hears the music of regiments
Loud in chorus, doctored with that medicine . . .

1977, *Jackpine Sonnets*. This book was a genuine return to form, in
more ways than one. It contained some of Acorn's best collected mate-
rial in ten years. Also, it saw him formalize the kind of unconventional
sonnet he'd been writing for decades. *Jackpine Sonnets* contains a
number of good poems and half a dozen exceptional ones. Acorn's
writing benefitted by being confined to the more rigorous strictures of
the sonnet form—even a free-form sonnet like the jackpine. It helped
him regain the control and focus that he had lost in the mid-seventies.

Acorn cited the nineteenth-century Canadian poet Archibald
Lampman as a direct inspiration for *Jackpine Sonnets*. He discovered
Lampman's writing in the fifties and recognized in it a true literary
antecedent to his own work. At times, Milton felt like a freak of
CanLit nature, an artist who came from nowhere and led to who-
knew-where. Writers like Lampman and Livesay helped him feel that
he was part of something better, an ongoing Canadian socialist poetry

tradition. It's easy to see why Lampman appealed to Milton; not only were the politics right (that is, left), but Lampman was an overlooked national treasure, whose best writing, like Acorn's, combined technical virtuosity with a simple passionate voice. To Acorn's mind, Lampman was yet another victim of the colonial forces that had subdued the country, a distinctive, and distinctly Canadian, voice who had been silenced by British and Yankee lords.

Untitled

On that beach with light shifting breaths
Of breezes touching us like gentle
Curious, strong, all-surrounding presences
Watching, and you watching;   I stuck a gull's
Tail feather, slanting ten white degrees
Out of perpendicular to match
The tilt of the nearest sail on that easy
-winded day.   Grief hope and fury
Were all there, speaking tentatively
In a jury just met: Wants too early
Stirring your blood, vision, nerves and mine
Over that tilting token in the sand;
Having made a sign, still wanted a sign
While low light blue waves just tapped the island.

––––––––––

October 1976, *Scarborough Fair*. A simple "jackpine sonnet," with a lot of complex things going on. Acorn has almost abandoned his usual rhetorical stance, and adopts the pose of the Romantic: despite its sonnet form, it's a kind of hybrid of his earlier lyric and short narrative work. It is an odd but successful mix that brings Acorn closer to postmodernism than he would ever have admitted. A different version of this poem appears in *Jackpine Sonnets* as "Love in the Nineteen Fifties."

E.T. Carbonell (1831–1929)

My momma's poppa, my grandpaw
Could take a turkey quill and cut a pen
Or anything with hands that he'd seen done
Although he was an English gentleman
Banished away for sundry offenses;
Sympathy for workers, other innocences.

Once his lip was shaven but grown back
On account of the rampant stiff upper lip
His moustache has pleasantly concealed.
Although he was a prime toff first and last
And never bothered to appear common
With all that conversational elegance;
Innate knack for the handling of men
He had an inappropriate love of justice;
Never too much good for his reputation.

His relatives would not accept title;
Genuine sprouts from the Welsh nobility
Such bowing would have lost them caste;
I don't know in who else's opinion.
He also was a man of principle,
In fact much too much principle for them.

It was lovely to watch his digits tie
A salmon fly, splice the main brace
In any sense you'd care to see him try,
Expression of an expert on his face.
I think he felt himself not inferior
To any worker in the matter of hands
So never had to bluff as superior;
And died, as do we most, a poor man.

Look at that albatross, up in the wind;
A living part of it, totally at ease,
Ready for any eventuality
As he was at repelling a robber,
Handling cutlery with such elegance
That he made eating a sheer act of grace:
By which he charmed my mother's mother Kate
At the age of sixty, when she was sixteen.

1981, unpublished. Another fine character study, never published before. It's from *The Bare-Eyed Birdwatcher*, a book Acorn often talked about in his later years but never completed.

The Completion of the Fiddle
(N.M.)

The fiddle's incomplete without the dance;
My darling. Let's hook fingers to complete
By motion to the calls, the sweet riddle
Of the tune now wriggling in the soft wind
On top of which the bright moon goes riding;
For if no happy bottoms prance and spin
Upon the planks and polish what's it all worth—
That round of steamed, shaped, rehardened wood
Varnished as it's put about a hollow
From which a tune may radiate its mirth
By the merry rub of gut against gut?
The candles flicker and the stars twinkle
All to be parts of the completed fiddle.

1982, *Captain Neal MacDougal & The Naked Goddess*. Acorn's sonnet
cycle is well-worth digging up in used bookstores. (He claimed that
most of the poems were dictated to him by spirit voices.) This joyous
poem ends the collection and is a fitting final word from a man who
only ever wanted to belong—not the fiddle, not the fiddler, but part of
the dance. A fire destroyed the publisher's copies of the book in which
this poem appears. James Deahl plans to bring out an expanded edition
in the near future.

It's All in Mother's Head
(*For Helen Carbonell Acorn, 1900-1984*)

It's all in mother's head that she can dance.
At seventy-nine that's just ridiculous.
But when the band commences purblind romance,
Spinning dizzy on a dizzy record,
Her eyes begin to burn and feet to tap.
Hands work an invisible accordion,
Till presently she's up with some assistance,
Like a tall ship heaving out its sails
Despite the wallops of the waves and tide
To convert the elements' resistance.

It's all in mother's head that she can glide
Unerringly through the erring couples.
All the able partners with whom she doubled
Are gone to ground or anchored to their chairs
Till she alone, to hand-applause and cheers,
Reels that are reels in every sense known—
Really doing it, still vast and full-blown,
Red-headed as ever a head was red.
Risen she is, but not from the dead;
From hopes that were false to hopes that are true,
From pert old-fashioned steps that seem to slide
As one cloud seems to coast upon another
In a cloggish and half-clumsy ride,
As a lupine bitch, leader of the pack,
Gets with each step just a whisht of a catch;
Sets each foot to raise it in all pride.

Each completed figure draws all breath
Out of a line of steam locomotives
Climbing the Rockies at a bawling crawl,

Or an ocean liner rolling all
The storm with it while fully figurative.
The eyes to watch her and the hands to catch
Would never let the floorboards hit her ass.
They fit too sure, are too well nailed for that:
Until after some moments she collapses
With a cry of, "How's that? How did I do?"
"Just fine our lady! Great-grandmother you!"
All in her head, but there's the evidence.

1986, *The Uncollected Acorn*. The last poem Acorn ever wrote, completed weeks before his death. It proves that, while the country might have given up on Milton Acorn, Milton Acorn had never given up on his craft.

Index